Four Supplications.

1529—1553 A.D.

Early English Text Society.

Extra Series. No. XIII.

BERLIN: ASHER & CO., 13, UNTER DEN LINDEN.
NEW YORK: C. SCRIBNER & CO.; LEYPOLDT & HOLT.
PHILADELPHIA: J. B. LIPPINCOTT & CO.

A Supplicacyon for the Beggers.

WRITTEN ABOUT THE YEAR 1529 BY

Simon Fish.

NOW RE-EDITED BY

FREDERICK J. FURNIVALL.

WITH

A Supplycacion to our moste Soueraigne Lorde Kynge Henry the Eyght

(1544 A.D.),

A Supplication of the Poore Commons

(1546 A.D.),

The Decaye of England by the great multitude of shepe

(1550-3 A.D.),

EDITED BY

J. MEADOWS COWPER.

LONDON:
PUBLISHED FOR THE EARLY ENGLISH TEXT SOCIETY
BY KEGAN PAUL, TRENCH, TRÜBNER & CO., LIMITED,
DRYDEN HOUSE, 43, GERRARD STREET, SOHO, W.
1871.

[*Reprinted 1891, 1905.*]

OXFORD
UNIVERSITY PRESS

Great Clarendon Street, Oxford OX2 6DP
United Kingdom

Oxford University Press is a department of the University of Oxford.
It furthers the University's objective of excellence in research, scholarship,
and education by publishing worldwide. Oxford is a registered trade mark of
Oxford University Press in the UK and in certain other countries

© The Early English Text Society 1871

The moral rights of the authors have been asserted

Database right Oxford University Press (maker)

First Edition published in 1871
Reprinted 1891, 1905, 2001

All rights reserved. No part of this publication may be reproduced,
stored in a retrieval system, or transmitted, in any form or by any means,
without the prior permission in writing of Oxford University Press,
or as expressly permitted by law, or under terms agreed with the appropriate
reprographics rights organization. Enquiries concerning reproduction
outside the scope of the above should be sent to the Rights Department,
Oxford University Press, at the address above

You must not circulate this book in any other form
and you must impose this same condition on any acquirer

Published in the United States of America by Oxford University Press
198 Madison Avenue, New York, NY 10016, United States of America

British Library Cataloguing in Publication Data
Data available

Library of Congress Cataloging in Publication Data
Data available

Extra Series, 13
ISBN 978-0-85-991958-6

FOREWORDS.

WHEN trying to get together some evidence on the Condition of England in Henry VIII's and Edward VI's reigns for the Introduction to the Ballad of *Now a Dayes* (? ab. 1520, A.D.) for my first volume for the Ballad Society, I was struck by the difficulty of finding out what tracts and books on the subject there were, and how few of them could be easily got at, much less bought at any reasonable price. But when I did get hold of some of them, I found them of such interest and value that I resolved to reprint such of them as I could, and one of the earliest[1] is now before the reader.

The second in date, the celebrated *Supplicacyon for the Beggers*, is however the first in importance, from its influence on Henry VIII and the Reformation, and its calling forth an answer from Sir Thomas More, his *Supplycacyon of Soulys* (in Purgatory), which gave rise to his controversy with Tyndal. I therefore give Foxe's full account of the whole matter from the third edition of his *Acts and Monuments*, A.D. 1576, pp. 986—991.

[1] Roy's *Rede me and be not wroth* is the earliest, and was in print by 1527 or -8, says Mr Arber. Mr Hazlitt dates Roy, 'Wormes 1526': but query. It is not in Foxe's list of Forbidden Books in 1526 (p. xii., below), though it is in that of 1531, printed in my *Political, Religious, and Love Poems*, 1866, p. 34 : '7. The burying of the masse in English yn ryme.' Of Roy's other book in that list, '13. A Boke made by freer Roye ayenst the sevyn sacramentis,' I know of no copy. Bohn's edition of Lowndes says of the '*Rede me and be not wroth*', "in the Roxburghe Sale Catalogue this piece stands entitled 'The Buryinge of the Mass, a Satire'." Can Foxe's 'M. Roo' on the next page be William Roy?

THE STORY OF M. SYMON FISHE.

M. Simon Fyshe, author of the booke, called the Supplication of Beggars.

Before the tyme of M. Bilney, and the fall of the Cardinall, I should haue placed the story of Symon Fish, with the booke called "the Supplication of Beggars," declaryng how and by what meanes it came to the kynges hand, and what effect therof followed after, in the reformation of many thynges, especially of the Clergy. But the missyng of a few yeares in this matter, breaketh no great square in our story, though it be now entred here [under the year 1531] which should haue come in sixe yeares before. The maner and circumstaunce of the matter is this:

After that the light of the Gospel, workyng mightely in Germanie, began to spread his beames here also in England, great styrre and alteration folowed in the harts of many: so that colored hypocrisie, and false doctrine, and painted holynes, began to be espyed more and more by the readyng of Gods word. The authoritie of the Bishop of Rome, and the glory of his Cardinals, was not so high, but such as had fresh wittes sparcled with Gods grace, began to espy Christ from Antichrist, that is, true sinceritie from counterfait religion. In the number of whom, was the sayd M. Symon Fish, a Gentleman of Grayes Inne. It happened the first yeare that this Gentleman came to London to dwell, which was about the yeare of our Lord .1525. that there was a certaine play or interlude made by one M. Roo of the same Inne, Gentleman, in which play partly was matter agaynst the Cardinal Wolsey. And where none durst take vpon them to play that part, whiche touched the sayd Cardinall, this foresayd M. Fish tooke vpon him to do it; wherupon great displeasure ensued agaynst him, vpon the Cardinals part: In so much as he, beyng pursued by the sayd Cardinall, the same night that this Tragedie was playd, was compelled of force to voyde his owne house, & so fled ouer the Sea vnto Tyndall: vpon occasion wherof, the next yeare folowyng this booke was made (beyng about the yeare .1527.) and so not long after, in the yeare (as I suppose) 1528. was sent ouer to the Lady Anne Bulleyne, who then lay at a place not farre from the Court. Which booke, her brother seyng in her hand, tooke it and read it, & gaue it her agayne, willyng her earnestly to giue it to the kyng, which thyng she so dyd.

Ex certa relatione, viuoque testimonio propriæ ipsius coniugis.

The booke of the supplication of beggars geuen to the kyng.

This was (as I gather) about the yeare of our Lord .1528. The kyng, after he had receaued the booke, demaunded of her, who made it. Wherunto she aunswered and sayd, a certaine subiect of his, one Fish, who was fled out of the Realme for feare of the Cardinall. After the kyng had kept the booke in his bosome iij. or iiij. dayes, as is credibly reported, such knowledge was giuen by the kynges seruantes to the wife of ye sayd Symon Fishe, y^t she might boldly send for her husband, without all perill or daunger. Whereupon, she thereby beyng incouraged, came first, and made sute to the kyng for the safe returne of her husband. Who, vnderstandyng whose wife she was, shewed a maruelous gentle nd chearefull countenaunce towardes her, askyng where her husband was. She aunswered, if it like your grace, not farre of. Then sayth he, fetch him, and he shall come and go safe without perill, and no man shal do him harme; saying moreouer that hee had much wrong that hee was from her so long: who had bene absent now the space of two yeares and a halfe. In the whiche meane tyme, the Cardinall was deposed, as is aforeshewed, and M. More set in his place of the Chauncellourshyp.

Thus Fishes wife, beyng emboldened by the kynges wordes, went immediatly to her husband beyng lately come ouer, and lying priuely within a myle of the Court, and brought him to the kyng: which appeareth to be about the yeare of our Lord .1530. When the kyng saw him, and vnderstode he was the authour of the booke, he came and embraced him with louing countenaunce; who after long talke, for the space of iij. or iiij. houres, as they were ridyng together on huntyng, at length dimitted him and bad him take home his wife, for she had taken great paynes for him. Who aunswered the kyng agayne and sayd, he durst not so do, for feare of Syr Thomas More, then Chauncellour, & Stoksley, then Byshop, of London. This seemeth to be about the yeare of our Lord .1530. _{M. Fishe brought, and gently entertayned of the kyng.}

The kyng, takyng his signet of his finger, willed hym to haue him recommended to the Lord Chauncellour, chargyng him not to bee so hardy to worke him any harme. M. Fishe, receiuyng the kynges signet, went and declared hys message to the Lord Chauncellour, who tooke it as sufficient for his owne discharge, but he asked him if he had any thyng for the discharge of his wife; for she a litle before had by chaunce displeased the Friers, for not sufferyng them to say their Gospels in Latine in her house, as they did in others, vnlesse they would say it in English. Whereupon the Lord Chauncellour, though he had discharged the man, yet leauyng not his grudge towardes the wife, the next mornyng sent his man for her to appeare before hym: who, had it not bene for her young daughter, which then lay sicke of the plague, had bene lyke to come to much trouble. Of the which plague her husband, the sayd M. Fish, deceasing within halfe a yeare, she afterward maryed to one M. Iames Baynham, Syr Alexander Baynhams sonne, a worshypful knight of Glostershyre. The which foresaid M. Iames Baynham, not long after was burned, as incontinently after, in the processe of this story, shall appeare.

And thus much concernyng Symon Fishe, the author of the booke of beggars, who also translated a booke called the Summe of the Scripture, out of the Dutch.

_{M. Fishe rescued by the kyng.}

_{Syr Tho. More persecuteth M. Fishes wyfe.}

_{M. Fishe dyeth of the plague.}

_{The summe of the scripture translated by M. Fishe.}

HOW THE 'SUPPLICACYON' GETS TO HENRY VIII.

Now commeth an other note of one Edmund Moddys, the kynges footeman, touchyng the same matter.

M. Moddys the kynges footeman. This M. Moddys beyng with the kyng in talke of religion, and of the new bookes that were come from beyond the seas, sayde, if it might please hys grace to pardon him, & such as he would bryng to his grace, hee should see such a booke as was maruell to heare of. The kyng demaunded what they were. *The booke of Beggars brought to the kyng by George Elyot, & George Robynson.* He sayd, two of your Marchauntes, George Elyot & George Robinson. The kyng poynted a tyme to speake with them. When they came afore his presence in a priuye closet, he demaunded what they had to saye, or to shew him. One of them said y^t there was a boke come to their hands, which they had there to shew his grace. When he saw it, hee demaunded if any of them could read it. Yea, sayd George Elyot, if it please your grace to heare it. I thought so, sayd the kyng, for if neede were, thou canst say it without booke.

The kynges aunswere vpon the booke of beggars. The whole booke beyng read out, the kyng made a long pause, and then sayd, if a man should pull downe an old stone wall and begyn at the lower part, the vpper part thereof might chaunce to fall vpon his head : and then he tooke the booke, and put it into his deske, and commaunded them vppon their allegiance, that they should not tell to any man, that he had sene the booke. &c. The Copie of the foresayd booke, intituled of the Beggars. here ensueth.

[The Boke of Beggars follows here in print.]

The supplication of the soules of Purgatory, made by Syr Tho. More, agaynst the booke of beggars. Agaynst this booke of the Beggers aboue prefixed, beyng written in the tyme of the Cardinall, another contrary booke or supplication, was deuised and written shortly upon the same by one sir Thomas More, knight, Chauncellour of the Duchy of Lancaster, vnder the name and title of the poore sely soules pewlyng out of Purgatory. In the which booke, after that the sayd M. More, writer therof, had first deuided the whole world into foure partes, that is, into heauen, hell, middle earth, and Purgatory : then he maketh the dead mens soules, by a Rhetoricall *Prosopopœa*, to speake out of Purgatory pynfolde, sometymes lamentably complayning, sometymes pleasauntly dalying and scoffing, at the authour of the Beggers booke, sometymes scoldyng and rayling at hym, callyng hym foole, witlesse, frantike, an asse, a goose, a madde dogge, an hereticke, and all that naught is. And no meruel, if these sely soules of Purgatory seeme so furnish & testy. For heate (ye know) is testie, & soone inflameth choler; but yet those Purgatory soules must take good hede how they call a man a foole and heretike so often. For if the sentence of the Gospell doth

Math. 5. pronounce them guiltie of hell fire, which say, *fatue*, foole : it may be douted lest those poore sely melancholy soules of

Purgatory, calling this man foole so oft as they haue done, do bryng themselues therby out of Purgatory fire, to the fire of hel, by ye iust sentence of the gospell: so that neyther the v. woundes of S. Fraunces, nor all the merites of S. Dominicke, nor yet of all the Friers, can release them, poore wretches. But yet for so much as I do not, nor cannot thincke, that those departed soules, eyther would so farre ouershoote themselues if they were in Purgatory, or els that there is any such fourth place of Purgatory at all (vnlesse it be in M. Mores Vtopia) as Maister Mores Poeticall vayne doth imagine. I cease therfore to burden the soules departed, and lay all the wyte in maister More, the authour and contriuer of this Poeticall booke, for not kepyng *Decorum Personæ*, as a perfect Poet should haue done. They that geue preceptes of Arte, do note thys in all Poeticall fictions, as a speciall obseruation, to foresee and expresse what is conuenient for euery person, accordyng to hys degree and condition, to speake and vtter. Wherefore if it be true that maister More sayeth in the sequele of hys booke, that grace and charitie increaseth in them that lye in the paynes of Purgatory, then is it not agreeable, that such soules, lying so long in Purgatory, should so soone forgette their charitie, and fall a rayling in their supplication so furnishly, both agaynst this man, with such opprobrious and vnfittyng termes, and also against Iohn Badby, Richard Howndon, Iohn Goose, Lord Cobham and other Martirs of the Lord burned for hys worde : also agaynst Luther, William Tindall, Richard Hunne and other mo, falsly belying the doctrine by them taught and defended : which is not lyke that such charitable soules of Purgatory would euer doe ; neyther were it conueniet for them in that case, which in dede though their doctrine were false, should redound to the more encrease of their payne. Agayne, where the B. of Rochester defineth the Angels to be ministers to Purgatory soules, some wyll thinke peraduenture maister More to haue missed some part of his *Decorum* in makyng the euill spirite of the authour and the deuill to be messenger betwene middle earth and Purgatory, in bringing tidinges to the prisoned soules, both of the booke, and of the name of the maker.

Vtopia, that is to say, *Nusquam*, no place.

A Poete sayth Horace. *Reddere personæ fit conuenientia cuique*

Now, as touchyng the maner how this deuill came into Purgatory, laughyng, grynnyng, and gnashyng his teeth, in sothe it maketh me to laugh, to see ye mery Antiques of M. More. Belike then this was some mery deuil, or els had eaten with his teeth some *Nasturcium* before : which comming into Purgatory to shew the name of this man, could not tell hys tale without laughing. But this was (sayth he) an enuious & an enuious laughing, ioyned with grynnyng and gnashyng of teeth. And immediatly vpon the same, was contriued this scoffing and raylyng supplication of the pewlyng soules of Purgatory, as hee hym selfe doth terme them. So then here was enuying, enuying, laugh-

M. Mores Antickes.

Satan *nasturciatur*.

ing, grinning, gnashyng of teeth, pewlyng, scoffing, rayling, and begging, and altogether to make a very blacke *Sanctus* in Purgatory.

A blacke Santus in Purgatory. In deede we read in Scripture, that there shall bee wepyng and gnashyng of teeth in hell, where the soules & bodyes of men shall be tormented. But who woulde euer haue thought before, that the euill aungell of this man that made the booke of Beggers, beyng a spirituall and no corporall substance, had teeth to gnashe, & a mouthe to grynne? But where then stode M. More, I meruell al this meane while, to see the deuill laugh with his mouth so wyde, yᵗ the soules of Purgatory might see all hys teeth? Belyke this was in Vtopia, where M. Mores Purgatorye is founded. But because M. Moore is hence departed, I will leaue hym with his mery Antiques. And as touchyng hys booke of Purgatory, whiche *The aunswere of Ioh. Frith against M. Mores purgatory.* he hath lefte behynde, because Iohn Frith hath learnedly and effectuously ouerthrowne the same, I will therfore referre the reader to hym, while I repayre agayne (the Lord willyng) to the historye.

After that the Clergye of England, and especially the Cardinall, vnderstode these bookes of the Beggars supplication aforesayd, to be strawne abroade in the streetes of London, and also before the kyng, the sayd Cardinall caused not onely his seruauntes diligently to attend to gather them vp, that they shoᵤ˙ l not come into the ḻ ynges handes, but also, when he vnderstode thaᵤ thᵉ kyng had receaued one or two of them, he came vnto the kynges Maiesty saying: If it shall please your grace, here are diuers seditious persons which haue scattered abroad books conteynyng manifest errours and herisies; desiryng his grace to beware of them. Wherupon the kyng, puttyng his hand in his bosome, tooke out one of the bookes, and deliuered it vnto the Cardinall. Then the Cardinall, together with the Byshops, consulted how they might prouide a spedy remedy for this mischief, *Prouision by the Byshops, agaynst Englishe bookes.* & therupon determined to geue out a Commision to forbid the readyng of all Englishe bookes, and namely this booke of Beggars, and the new Testament of Tyndals translation: which was done out of hand by Cuthbert Tonstall, Byshop of London, who sent out his prohibition vnto his Archdeacons, with all spede, for the forbiddyng of that booke and diuers other more; the tenor of whiche prohibition here foloweth.

¶ A prohibition sent out by Cuthbert Tonstall,
Bishop of London, to the Archdeacons of his diocesse, for the callyng in of the new Testaments
translated into English, with diuers
other bokes: the Cataloge wherof hereafter ensueth.

A prohibition against English bookes. "CVthbert by the permission of God, Byshop of London, vnto our welbeloued in Christ, the Archdeacon of London, or to hys Officiall, health, grace, and benediction. By the duety of our pastorall office, we are bounde diligently with all our power, to foresee, prouide for, roote out, and put away, all those thynges which seeme to tend to the peril & daunger of our subiectes, and specially the destruction of their soules. Wherefore, we, hauyng vnderstandyng by the report of diuers credible persons, and also by the euident apparaunce of the matter, that many children of iniquitie, maintayners of Luthers sect, blynded through extreme wickednes, wandryng from the way of truth and the Catholicke fayth, craftely haue translated the new Testament into our English tongue, entermedlyng therwith many hereticall Articles & erroneous opinions, pernicious and offensiue, seducyng the simple people, attemptyng by their wicked and peruerse interpretations, to prophanate the maiestye of the Scripture, which hetherto hath remained vndefiled, & craftely to abuse the most holy worde of God, and the true sence of the same; of the which translation there are many bookes imprinted, some with gloses and some without, contayning in the English tongue that pestiferous and most pernicious poyson dispersed throughout all our diocesse of London in great number: which truly, without it be spedely foreseene, wythout doubt, wyll contaminate and infect the flock committed vnto us, with most deadly poyson and heresie, to the grieuous peril and danger of the soules committed to our charge, and the offence of gods diuine maiesty. Wherfore we, Cuthbert the bishop aforesayd, greuously sorowyng for the premisses, willyng to withstand the craft and subtletie of the auncient enemy and hys ministers, which seeke the destruction of my flock, and with a diligent care, to take hede vnto the flock committed to my charge, desiring to prouide spedy remedies for the premisses, do charge you ioyntly and seuerally, & by vertue of your obedience, straightly enioyne and commaunde you, that by our authority you warne or cause to be warned all & singular, aswel exempt as not exempt, dwelling within your Archdeaconries, that within .xxx. dayes space, wherof .x. dayes shalbe for the first, .x. for the second, & .x. for the third and peremptory terme, vnder paine of excommunication, and incurring the suspicion of herisie, they do bryng in, and really deliuer vnto our vicare generall, all & singular such bookes as conteyne the translation of the new Testament in the Englishe tongue; and that you doe certifie vs, or our sayd Commissarye, within ij. monethes after the day of the date of these presentes, duely, personally, or by your letters, together with these presentes, vnder your seales, what you haue done in the premisses, vnder payne of contempt, geuen vnder our seale the .xxiij. of October, in the v. yere of our consecration .an. 1526."

¶ The lyke Commission in lyke maner and forme, was sent to the three other Archdeacons of Middlesexe, Essex, and Colchester, for the execution of the same matter, vnder the Byshops seale.

THE NAMES OF THE BOOKES THAT WERE FORBIDDEN AT THIS TYME, TOGETHER WITH THE NEW TESTAMENT.

Bookes con-
demned and
forbidden.

THe supplication of beggers.	(2)[1]
The reuelation of Antichrist, of Luther.	(3)
The new Testament of Tindall.	(22)
The wicked Mammon.	(23)
The obedience of a Christen man.	(24)
An introduction to Paules Epistle to the Romanes.	(22)
A Dialogue betwixt the father and the sonne.	(1)
Oeconomicæ Christianæ.	(6)
Vnio dissidentium.	
Piæ precationes.	(5)
Captiuitas Babilonica.	
Ioannes Hus in Oseam.	
Zwinglius in Catabaptistas.	
De pueris instituendis.	
Brentius de administranda Republica.	
Luther ad Galatas.	
De libertate Christiana.	
Luthers exposition vpon the Pater noster.	

The editor of the reprint of the *Supplicacyon* in 1845 refers also to Strype's *Memorials*, i. 165, and says that Wilkins (*Concilia*, 3. 706) gives us this edict or injunction [of Tonstall's, above] issued by the authority also of Warham, Archbishop of Canterbury. Again, in the year 1530, a public instrument agreed upon, says Wilkins (3. 728), in an Assembly of the Archbishop of Canterbury, the Bishop of Durham and others, by order of King Henry the Eighth, was put forth "containing divers heretical and erroneous opinions selected from various books, which had been considered and condemned." One of those is from *the Supplication*, and is the passage [on Purgatory] beginning, "There be many men of great literature, &c." [p. 10, below, l. 21], and ending, "in all holy Scripture." And, once more, in the same year (*Wilkins*, iii. 737), or, with less probability, in 1529 (*Strype*, i. 165), a Royal Proclamation was published "for resisting and withstanding of most damnable heresies sown

---

[1] These numbers refer to those in the 'List of Books proscribed in 1531' printed in my edition of *Political, Religious, and Love Poems*, for the Society, 1866, p. 34-5, in which nine books in Tonstall's 1526 list are repeated. (The *Pre* of No. 5 there should be *Pie*.)

within this realm by the disciples of Luther, and other heretics, perverters of Christ's religion;" at the end of which, with some other books, "the Supplication of Beggars" is strictly prohibited. Mr Arber tells me that Foxe's list of books on the opposite page is a spurious one, because it contains the names of several books not publisht till after 1526,—among them our *Supplication of Beggars*, which can be proved to have been publisht late in 1528 or early in 1529[1];—that the *Unio dissidentium* is by H. Budius; and that *Piæ Precationes, Captivitas Babylonica*, and *De Libertate Christiana*, are Luther's.

Wood's account of Fish, in his *Athenæ Oxonienses*, is taken from Foxe, but he notes also what Sir T. More, in his 'Apology' (*Works*, &c., ed. Rastell, 1577, p. 881), says of Fish: that he "had good zele, ye wote well, whan he made the Supplicacion of beggers. But God gaue hym suche grace afterwarde, *that* he was sory for that good zeale, *and* repented hymselfe, and came into the church agayne; and forsoke and forsware all the whole hill of those heresyes, out of which the fountain of that same good zeale sprange."

"In More's *Supplication of Souls*, written to counteract the effect of Mr Simon Fish's *Supplication of Beggars*, More continually calls Fish 'this beggar's proctor,' and represents one of the souls in purgatory as saying of him, 'He is named and boasted among us by the evil angel of his, our and your ghostly enemy, the devil; which, as soon as he had set him at work with that pernicious book, ceased not to come hither, and boast it among us: but with his enmious and envious laughter, gnashing the teeth and grinning, he told us that his people [*i. e.* the reformers] had, by the advice and counsel of him, [*i. e.* the devil] and of some heretics almost as evil as he, made such a book for beggars, that it should make us beg long ere we got aught.'—*More's 'Works,'* pp. 288-9. The *Supplication of Beggars* . . . . was originally transmitted to England from the Continent, whither Fish had fled; so that More would suppose that Tyndale and Joye were privy to its composition."—*Parker Soc.'s Tyndale's 'Works,'* iii. 268, note. In the Parker Society's Tyndale's Works, ii. 335, Tyndale, in his tract on *The Practice of Prelates*, again makes mention of Fish's *Supplication*, "which secretary (Thomas More) yet must first deserve it with writing against Martin [Luther], and

---

[1] See Mr Arber's Preface to his facsimile reproduction (1871) of Tyndale and Roy's first printed English New Testament, Cologne-Worms? 1525, 4to.

against *The Obedience* and *Mammon,* and become the proctor of purgatory, to write against *The Supplication of beggars.*"

Bishop Tanner ascribes to Fish 'The boke of merchants[1] rightly necessary to all folkes, newly made by the lord Pontapole,' and 'The spiritual nosegay.'
That he translated from the Dutch the *Sum of the Scriptures* Foxe has already told us in the last lines of page vii above.
Fish was living at his house at Whitefriars in 1527-8. See Necton's Confession. *Strype,* I. ii. 63, ed. 1822. (Arber.)
No new facts about Fish are given in any modern biographical dictionaries that Mr W. M. Wood has searched for me. Foxe, as we have seen (p. vii, above, l. 9 from foot), says that Fish died of the plague about 1530 ; and the way that Sir Thomas More speaks of him seems to assume that he died before 1533.
The reader will notice how the *Supplication of the Poore Commons,* 1546, refers, on p. 61-2 below, to the *Supplicacyon of Beggers,* and its influence on Henry VIII.

F. J. F.

The second and third *Supplications,* printed from the original black-letter editions now in the British Museum,[2] are anonymous. The dates of their publication are 1544 for the second, and 1546 for the third. It is useless to guess who was the author (I believe the two proceed from one pen), but I have not much hesitation in suggesting Henry Brinklow (" Roderyck Mors "), who was busy at this time. Brinklow's two tracts[3] will as soon as practicable be included in this series, and then our readers will be able to judge for themselves. The same vehement language, and unqualified abuse of the clergy and all who were not of his way of thinking, will be observed throughout. The references to certain topics of the day cannot be

[1] Lond. Jugge, 1547, 12mo.—*Lowndes.*
[2] Mr E. Brock read the proofs with the originals.
[3] 'The Complaynt of Roderyck Mors . . . for the redresse of certen wicked lawes, euel customs, and cruel decreys, 1536 '; and 'The Lamentacyon of a Christen Agaynst the Cytye of London, for some certayne great vyces vsed therin, 1545.

THE SECOND AND THIRD SUPPLICATIONS.

reckoned on to weigh much with regard to the question of authorship in a case like this, else we might direct attention to several such in this Preface. Three must suffice:

The Lamentacyon of a Christen.
And I thinke within fewe years they will (wythout thy greate mercy) call vpon Thomas Wolsey late Cardinall, & vpon the vnholy (I shulde saye) holy Mayde of Kent. l. 4.
Accordyng to there office they barked vppon you to loke vppon the poore, so that then some relefe they had; but now, alasse, ye be colde, yea euen those whiche saye they be the favorers of the Gospell. l. 9, bk.
London beyng one of the flowers of the worlde, as touchinge worldlye riches, hath so manye, yea innumerable of poore people forced to go from dore to dore, and to syt openly in the stretes a beggynge, and many . . . . lye in their howses . . . . and dye for lacke of ayde of the riche. l. 9.
Ye abhorre the remedy ordayned of God [marriage], and mayntayne the remedy of Sathan. l. 22, bk.

A Supplication of the Commons.
Now must we beleue that they can not erre . . . . . . though they were baudes and fornicators with the holy whore of Kent. p. 75.

Although the sturdy beggers gat all the deuotion of the good charitable people from them, yet had the pore impotent creatures sone relefe of theyr scrappes, where as nowe they haue nothyng. Then had they hospitals, and almeshouses to be lodged in, but nowe they lye and starue in the stretes. Then was their number great, but now much greater. p. 79.

Hordome is more estemed then wedlocke . . . amongest a great numbre of lycensious persons. p. 82.

These are not worth much, but they may serve as a hint to those who care to go further in this direction.

The subjects embraced by the second and third *Supplications* are such as to justify their being placed in the same volume as Fish's more famous tract.[1] That gained its celebrity as much from its early appearance in the great struggle, and the notice taken of it by the king, as by its own intrinsic merits. More than this, Foxe embalmed it in his

[1] When the *Supplication of the Poore Commons* first appeared, it bore on its title page "¶ Whereunto is added the Supplication of Beggers." This is now omitted, as the *Supplication of Beggars* contained in the present volume is printed from a copy of the original black-letter edition in the British Museum.

pages, so that while the *Supplication to the King* and the *Supplication of the Commons* have not been reprinted for more than 300 years, and are unknown except to a few, the *Supplication of the Beggers* has been reproduced as often as Foxe's own immortal work.

The ignorance and immorality of the clergy are commented upon in severe terms. They, as usual, are charged with being the authors of every crime either by the suppression of the Bible, or by their false teaching. Their want of faith and neglect of preaching are said to be the cause of insurrections, commotions, popish blindness, idolatry, hypocrisy. It is said that many of the Abbots of the suppressed monasteries were admitted to have the cure of souls to the increase of all ignorance and to the damnation of those committed to their care. Of course. Having turned out these men, how could the virtuous patriots of the day do less than persecute them to the death? They had voluntarily or involuntarily resigned their livings into the hands of the Royal Defender of the Faith, and were willing to conform to the new order of things; but this was not enough. It was held that no good thing could come out of the Church as it existed a few years before, and so these men must submit to every indignity and be taxed with every crime. It was even considered dangerous to admit a man to the ministry who had studied the decrees and laws of the Church of Rome (p. 46).

But Church matters are not the only ones which gain attention. We hear of the extravagance which prevailed in fashions—now the French, now the Spanish, then the Italian, and then the Milan (p. 52), till many were brought to poverty by the foolish fancies and vain pride of men and women. The crimes of the rich make the writer apply Hosea's words to his own country—" There is no truth, no mercy, no knowledge of God in earth; cursing, lying, murder, theft, adultery, hath broken in "—and yet, notwithstanding all this, " doo owre shepherdes holde theyr peace."

The miserable poverty of the people, who expected great things from the expulsion of the monks, is clearly expressed. Under the old order of things there was some relief (p. 79), but under the new, instead of the monk there was the " sturdy extortioner." The people could get no farm, not even a cottage. Rents were raised, abbey lands bought up, and the old leases declared to be void. Altogether the picture is anything but a cheering one, and makes us curious to know in what part of England "free fare and free lodging, with bread, beef, and beer," were to be had, and no questions asked.[1]

The last tract in this volume was copied from one then in the Lambeth Library, but as that was mislaid when we went to press, our text has been made to correspond[2] with the copy of another edition in the Cambridge University Library. The date[3] of this "Sheep-tract" must be 1550-3 A.D.; but the name of its author is unknown. It, too, is in the form of a petition or supplication, which seems to have been a favourite mode of exposing the grievances under which the people groaned. A noteworthy circumstance in connection with this tract is that the clergy are not even mentioned! It deals with rural troubles only. In cities men saw and perhaps envied the rich; in large centres of population also, just as in our own day, the clergy were the especial objects of the attacks of "reformers;" but this writer, whose style is far less effective than that of the *Supplications*, confines himself solely to the misfortunes which resulted from excessive pasture farming. His references to Northamptonshire, Buckinghamshire, and Oxfordshire, lead us to believe that his lot was probably cast in one of these counties. The complaint is made in very homely language and manner, but they give to it an air of truthfulness.

The calculations as to the losses sustained by the country are very interesting. A single plow, it seems, was calculated to keep six persons and leave thirty quarters of grain for sale annually.

[1] For further information on the subjects of these Supplications the reader is referred to the Introduction to *Ballads from MSS*, vol. i. by Mr F. J. Furnivall, and to the Preface to *England under Henry VIII., a Dialogue*, &c., by Mr J. M. Cowper.

[2] Mr Denis Hall of the Camb. Univ. Library collated the proofs with the original.

[3] Hugh Singleton's print of *The vocacyon of Johan Bale* is dated 1553, and he died between July 1592 and 1593. Herbert gives the date of Singleton's ed. of Fox's *Instruccion of Christen Fayth* as 1550. (Dibdin's Ames, iv. 290.) The copy of the Sheep-Tract mentioned in Ames as among the Harleian pamphlets is not now in the British Museum. It was the same edition as the missing Lambeth copy, having an *e* in *onely* and *housholde* in the title.—F.

Put into figures, the first calculation (p. 98) will stand thus:—

40 plows decayed in each county:
1 plow = 6 persons ∴ 40 plows = 240 persons.
In addition each plow yielded 30 qrs. corn. ∴ 40 plows = 1200 qrs. Allowing 4 qrs. to each person, this shows a further loss of <u>300</u> „

Total in each county 540 „

But if there be 80 plows less in each of these shires, "as we do think" (p. 99), this number will be doubled, and in each county 1080 persons are deprived of their means of support.[1] In the writer's own touching language we may say, "Now these persons had need to have living: whither shall they go? into Northamptonshire? And there is also the living of an equal number of persons lost. Whither shall then they go? Forth from shire to shire, and to be scattered thus abroad, within the King's Majesty's Realm where it shall please Almighty God; and for lack of masters, by compulsion driven, some of them to beg, and some to steal" (p. 98).

These Reformation Tracts are submitted to the careful attention of all who wish to study this period of our history, in the firm belief that the only way in which Englishmen can form a correct estimate of the wonderful change the country then went through, the causes which led to it, and the means by which it was brought about, is by placing in their hands all the contemporary documents which are within our reach.

J. M. COWPER.

[1] The calculation on p. 101 suggests a condition of things too frightful for belief:

1 Plow kept 6 persons
besides producing corn sufficient for $7\frac{1}{2}$ „
50,000 plows × $13\frac{1}{2}$ = 675,000 „

thrown upon the country; which, supposing the population to have been 5,000,000, would be one-eighth of the whole population, and reveals a state of things worse than that which exists at the present day, when every twentieth person receives parish relief, exclusive of the "beggars" who swarm on our highways, tramping from Union to Union because they can't sleep in the same "house" two nights together.

A Supplicacyon for the Beggers.

WRITTEN ABOUT THE YEAR 1529,

AND (AS IS BELIEVED) BY

Simon Fish.

NOW RE-EDITED BY

FREDERICK J. FURNIVALL.

TO THE KING OVRE

souereygne lorde.

MOst lamentably compleyneth theyre wofull mysery vnto youre highnes, youre poore daily bedemen, the wretched hidous monstres (on whome scarcely for horror any yie dare loke,) the foule, vnhappy sorte of lepres, and other sore people, nedy, impotent, blinde, lame, and sike, that live onely by almesse, howe that theyre nombre is daily so sore encreased, that all the almesse of all the weldisposed people of this youre realme is not halfe ynough for to susteine theim, but that for verey constreint they die for hunger. And this most pestilent mischief is comen vppon youre saide poore beedmen, by the reason and[1] there is, yn the tymes of youre noble predecessours passed, craftily crept ynto this your realme an other sort (not of impotent, but) of strong, puissaunt, and counterfeit holy, and ydell, beggers and vacabundes, whiche, syns the tyme of theyre first entre by all the craft and wilinesse of Satan, are nowe encreased vnder your sight, not onely into a great nombre, but also ynto a kingdome. These are (not the herdes, but the rauinous wolues going in herdes clothing, deuouring the flocke,) the Bisshoppes, Abbottes, Priours, Deacons, Archedeacons, Suffraganes, Prestes, Monkes, Chanons, Freres, Pardoners and Somners. And who is abill to nombre this idell,

Marginalia: The King's beadsmen, though lepers, maimed, and blind, find not half enough alms to sustain them; and this by reason that others who are [1 *for that*] strong and able have crept in, numerous enough to form a kingdom. These are no shepherds, but wolves, that is, Bishops, Abbots, &c.,

2   THE EXTORTIONS OF THE MONKS AND FRIARS.

who work not, but have the third of the land in their hands;

rauinous sort, whiche (setting all laboure a side) haue begged so importunatly that they haue gotten ynto theyre hondes more then the therd part of all youre Realme. The goodliest lordshippes, maners, londes,

with the tithe of corn and wool, &c.,

and territories, are theyrs. Besides this, they haue the tenth part of all the corne, medowe, pasture, grasse, wolle, coltes, calues, lambes, pigges, gese, and chikens.

and of every servant's wages,

Ouer and bisides, the tenth part of euery seruauntes wages, the tenth part of the wolle, milke, hony, waxe, chese, and butter. Ye, and they loke so narowly vppon

as well as the good-woman's eggs, or else she has no Easter rights.

theyre proufittes, that the poore wyues must be countable to theym of euery tenth eg, or elles she gettith not her ryghtes at ester, shalbe taken as an heretike. hereto

Then, they gain much by probates, private tithes and masses,

haue they theire foure offering daies. whate money pull they yn by probates of testamentes, priuy tithes, and by mennes offeringes to theyre pilgremages, and at theyre first masses? Euery man and childe that is buried, must pay sumwhat for masses and diriges to be

for which dead men's friends must pay; and from confessions (which they divulge), from cursing and absolving..

song for him, or elles they will accuse the dedes frendes and executours of heresie. whate money get they by mortuaries, by hearing of confessions (and yet they wil kepe therof no counceyle) by halowing of churches, altares, superaltares, chapelles, and belles, by cursing of men, and absoluing theim agein for money? what a multitude of money gather the pardoners in a yere? Howe moche money get the Somners by extorcion yn a yere, by assityng the people to the commissaries court, and afterward releasing thapparaunce for money?

Then again, how great is the number of the begging Friars.

Finally, the infinite nombre of begging freres: whate get they yn a yere? Here, if it please your grace to marke, ye shall se a thing farre out of ioynt. There are withyn youre realme of Englond .lij. thousand parisshe

In England are 52,000 parish churches, 10 households in each parish;

churches. And this stonding, that there be but tenne houshouldes yn euery parisshe, yet are there fiue hundreth thousand and twenty thousand houshouldes.

from each household the

And of euery of these houshouldes hath euery of the

A SUPPLICACYON FOR THE BEGGERS.

fiue ordres of freres a peny a quarter for euery ordre, that is, for all the fiue ordres, fiue pens a quarter for every house. That is, for all the fiue ordres .xx. d, a yere of euery house. Summa, fiue hundreth thousand and twenty thousand quarters of angels. That is .cclx. thousand half angels. Summa .cxxx. thousand angels. Summa totalis .xliij. thousand poundes and .cccxxxiij. li. vi.s. viij.d. sterling. wherof not foure hundreth yeres passed they had not one peny. Oh greuous and peynfull exactions thus yerely to be paied! from the whiche the people of your nobill predecessours, the kinges of the auncient Britons, euer stode fre. And this wil they haue, or els they wil procure him that will not giue it theim to be taken as an heretike. whate tiraunt euer oppressed the people like this cruell and vengeable generacion? whate subiectes shall be abill to helpe theire prince, that be after this facion yerely polled? whate good christen people can be abill to socoure vs pore lepres, blinde, sore, and lame, that be thus yerely oppressed? Is it any merueille that youre people so compleine of pouertie? Is it any merueile that the taxes, fiftenes, and subsidies, that your grace most tenderly of great compassion hath taken emong your people, to defend theim from the thretened ruine of theire comon welth, haue bin so sloughtfully, ye, painfully leuied? Seing that almost the vtmost peny that mought haue bin leuied, hath ben gathered bifore yerely by this rauinous, cruell, and insatiabill generacion. The danes, nether the saxons, yn the time of the auncient Britons, shulde neuer haue ben abill to haue brought theire armies from so farre hither ynto your lond, to haue conquered it, if they had had at that time suche a sort of idell glotons to finde at home. The nobill king Arthur had neuer ben abill to haue caried his armie to the fote of the mountaines, to resist the coming downe of lucius the Emperoure, if suche

fiue orders take 20 pence a year, or in round numbers, £43,333 6s. 8d.

Your Highness's predecessors did not pay this, and

no subiects can help their king if they are so fleeced; and none can giue alms to us.

How will the taxes, which you have so tenderly taken, be levied? for these raveners have got all beforehand.

Neither Dane nor Saxon could have won Britain, if they had had such a brood at home.

Nor could Arthur have resisted Lucius, with such extortioners

THE FEW MONKS, ETC., HAVE HALF THE REALM.

among his people, nor the Greeks besieged Troy,

yerely exactions had ben taken of his people. The grekes had neuer ben abill to haue so long continued at the siege of Troie, if they had had at home suche an idell sort of cormorauntes to finde. The auncient

nor Rome won the world, nor the Turk so much of Christendom.

Romains had neuer ben abil to haue put all the hole worlde vnder theyre obeisaunce, if theyre people had byn thus yerely oppressed. The Turke nowe, yn youre tyme, shulde neuer be abill to get so moche grounde of cristendome, if he had yn his empire suche a sort of

These men, then, have nigh half the substance of the realm,

locustes to deuoure his substaunce. Ley then these sommes to the forseid therd part of the possessions of the realme, that ye may se whether it drawe nighe vnto the half of the hole substaunce of the realme or not: So shall ye finde that it draweth ferre aboue. Nowe let vs then compare the nombre of this vnkind idell sort, vnto the nombre of the laye people, and we shall se whether it be indifferently shifted or not that they

and yet they are but one in a hundred of the lay-men, or with women and children added, one in four;

shuld haue half. Compare theim to the nombre of men, so are they not the .C. person. Compare theim to men, wimen, and children; then are they not the .CCCC. parson yn nombre. One part therfore, yn foure hundreth partes deuided, were to moche for theim

but yet they have half the property of the realm.

except they did laboure. whate an vnequal burthen is it, that they haue half with the multitude, and are not the .CCCC. parson of theire nombre! whate tongue is abill to tell that euer there was eny comon welth so sore oppressed sins the worlde first began?

What do they with their exactions? Nothing, but claim all power; excite rebellions, as they did

¶ And whate do al these gredy sort of sturdy, idell, holy theues, with these yerely exactions that they take of the people? Truely nothing but exempt theim silues from thobedience of your grace. Nothing but translate all rule, power, lordishippe, auctorite, obedience, and dignite, from your grace vnto theim. Nothing but that all your subiectes shulde fall ynto disobedience and rebellion ageinst your grace, and be vnder theym. As they did vnto your nobill predecessour king Iohn : whiche, forbicause that he wolde haue *against that noble King John, when one of them interdicted the land;* punisshed certeyr traytours that had conspired with the frenche king to haue deposed him from his crowne and dignite, (emoug the whiche a clerke called Stephen, whome afterward ageinst the kinges' will the Pope made Bisshoppe of Caunterbury, was one) enterdited his Lond. For the whiche mater your most nobill realme wrongfully (alas, for shame !) hath stond tributary (not vnto any kind temporall prince, but vnto a cruell, deuelisshe bloudsupper, dronken in the bloude of the sayntes and marters of christ) euer sins. Here were an holy sort of prelates, that thus cruelly coude punisshe suche a rightuous kinge, all his realme, and succession, for doing right ! *and from that time the land has been tributary to a devilish bloodsupper. A holy sort of prelates to treat a righteous king so!*

¶ Here were a charitable sort of holy men, that coude thus enterdite an hole realme, and plucke awey thobedience of the people from theyre naturall liege lorde and kinge, for none other cause but for his rightuousnesse! Here were a blissed sort, not of meke herdes, but of bloudsuppers, that coude set the frenche king vppon suche a rightuous prince, to cause hym to lose his crowne and dignite, to make effusion of the bloude of his people, oneles this good and blissed king of greate compassion, more fearing and lamenting the sheding of the bloude of his people then the losse of his crowne and dignite, agaynst all right and conscience had submitted him silf vnto theym ! O case most horrible ! that euer so nobill a king, Realme, and succession, shuide thus be made to stoupe to suche a sort of bloudsuppers ! where was his swerde, power, crowne, and dignite become, wherby he mought haue done iustice yn this maner? where was their obedience become, that shuld haue byn subiect vnder his highe power yn this mater? Ye, where was the obedience of all his subiectes become, that for maintenaunce of the comon welth shulde haue holpen him manfully to haue re- *Holy men were they! hating one who more feared to shed blood than lose his crown; but they had translated all power to themselves.*

sisted these bloudsuppers to the shedinge of theyre bloude? was not all to-gither by theyre polycy translated from this good king vnto theim? Ye, and what do they more? Truely nothing but applie theym silues, by all the sleyghtes they may, to haue to do with euery mannes wife, euery mannes doughter, and euery mannes mayde, that cukkoldrie and baudrie shulde reigne ouer all emong your subiectes, that noman shulde knowe his owne childe, that theyre bastardes might enherite the possessions of euery man, to put the right begotten children clere beside theire inheritaunce, yn subuersion of all estates and godly ordre. These be they that by theire absteyning from mariage do let the generation of the people, wherby all the realme at length, if it shulde be continued, shall be made desert and inhabitable.[1]

No man's wife or daughter is safe for them; so that no man can be sure of his own child; and still by abstaining from marriage, they may make the realm desolate.

¶ These be they that haue made an hundreth thousand ydell hores yn your realme, whiche wolde haue gotten theyre lyuing honestly, yn the swete of theyre faces, had not theyre superfluous rychesse illected theym to vnclene lust and ydelnesse. These be they that corrupt the hole generation of mankind yn your realme; that catche the pokkes of one woman, and bere theym to an other; that be brent wyth one woman, and bere it to an other; that catche the lepry of one woman, and bere it to an other; ye, some one of theym shall bost emong his felawes, that he hath medled with an hundreth wymen. These be they that when they haue ones drawen mennes wiues to suche incontinency, spende awey theire husbondes goodes, make the wimen to runne awey from theire husbondes, ye, rynne awey them silues both with wif and goodes, bring both

But for them, 100,000 women would have lived honestly.

They carry disease from one to another, and boast of their success.

They draw women from their husbands.

---

[1] Sir Thomas More points out the seeming contradiction between this sentence and the last: for if the monks were such good begetters of bastards, they would increase the population, rather than diminish it. But this is answered in the next page here.

man, wife, and children, to ydelnesse, theft, and beggeri.

Ye, who is abill to nombre the greate and brode botomles occean see, full of euilles, that this mischeuous and sinful generacion may laufully bring vppon vs vnponisshed? where is youre swerde, power, crowne, and dignite become, that shuld punisshe (by punisshement of deth, euen as other men are punisshed) the felonies, rapes, murdres, and treasons committed by this sinfull generacion? where is theire obedience become, that shulde be vnder your hyghe power yn this mater? ys not all to-gither translated and exempt from your grace vnto theim? yes, truely. whate an infinite nombre of people might haue ben encreased, to haue peopled the realme, if these sort of folke had ben maried like other men? whate breche of matrimonie is there brought yn by theim? suche truely as was neuer, sins the worlde began, emong the hole multitude of the hethen.

¶ Who is she that wil set her hondes to worke, to get .iij. d. a day, and may haue at lest .xx. d. a day to slepe an houre with a frere, a monke, or a prest? what is he that wolde laboure for a grote a day, and may haue at lest .xij. d. a day to be baude to a prest, a monke, or a frere? whate a sort are there of theime that mari prestes souereigne ladies, but to cloke the prestes yncontinency, and that they may haue a liuing of the prest theime silues for theire laboure? Howe many thousandes doth suche lubricite bring to beggery, theft, and idelnesse, whiche shuld haue kept theire good name, and haue set theim silues to worke, had not ben this excesse treasure of the spiritualtie? whate honest man dare take any man or woman yn his seruice that hath ben at suche a scole with a spiritual man? Oh the greuous shipwrak of the comon welth, whiche yn auncient time, bifore the coming yn of these rauinous

Why should you not punish them as you do other men?

Evils numberless they bring on us.

Why should they not be married like other men?

What woman will work for 3d. a day, when she may get 20d. by sleeping with a monk?

How many men marry priests' ladies, just to get a living by it?

Before these wolves came,

wolues, was so prosperous, that then there were but fewe theues! ye, theft was at that tyme so rare, that Cesar was not compellid to make penalite of deth vppon felony, as your grace may well perceyue yn his institutes. There was also at that tyme but fewe pore people, and yet they did not begge, but there was giuen theim ynough vnaxed; for there was at that time none of these rauinous wolues to axe it from theim, as it apperith yn the actes of thappostles. Is it any merueill though there be nowe so many beggers, theues, and ydell people? Nay truely.

¶ Whate remedy: make lawes ageynst theim? I am yn doubt whether ye be able: Are they not stronger in your owne parliament house then your silfe? whate a nombre of Bisshopes, abbotes, and priours, are lordes of your parliament? are not all the lerned men in your realme in fee with theim, to speake yn your parliament house for theim ageinst your crowne, dignite, and comon welth of your realme; a fewe of youre owne lerned counsell onely excepted? whate lawe can be made ageinst theim that may be aduaylable? who is he (though he be greued never so sore) for the murdre of his auncestre, rauisshement of his wyfe, of his doughter, robbery, trespas, maiheme, dette, or eny other offence, dare ley it to theyre charge by any wey of accion? and if he do, then is he by and by, by theyre wilynesse, accused of heresie. ye, they will so handle him or he passe, that except he will bere a fagot for theyre pleasure, he shal be excommunicate, and then be all his accions dasshed. So captyue are your lawes vnto theym, that no man that they lyst to excommunicat, may be admitted to sue any accion in any of your courtes. If eny man yn your sessions dare be so hardy to endyte a prest of eny suche cryme, he hath, or the yere go out, suche a yoke of heresye leyd in his necke, that it maketh him wisshe that he had not done it. Your grace may se whate a worke there is in London, howe the bisshoppe rageth for endyting of certayn curates of extorcion and incontinency, the last yere in the warmoll quest.¹ Had not Richard hunne commenced accyon of premunire ageinst a prest, he had bin yet alyue, and none eretik, a tall, but an honest man. [*as your Grace has seen, because certain curates were charged with incontinency. Take Richard Hunne's case.*]

¶ Dyd not dyuers of your noble progenitours,— seynge theyre crowne and dignite runne ynto ruyne, and to be thus craftely translated ynto the hondes of this myscheuous generacyon,—make dyuers statutes for the reformacyon therof, emong whiche the statute of mortmayne was one? to the intent that after that tyme they shulde haue no more gyuen vnto theim. [*Did not your ancestors pass the statute of mortmain against them?*]

But whate avayled it? haue they not gotten ynto theyre hondes, more londes sins, then eny duke yn ynglond hath, the statute notwithstonding? Ye, haue they not for all that translated ynto theyre hondes, from your grace, half your kyngdome thoroughly? The hole name, as reason is, for the auncientie of your kyngdome, whiche was bifore theyrs, and out of the whiche theyrs is growen, onely abiding with your grace? and of one kyngdome made tweyne : the spirituall kyngdome (as they call it), for they wyll be named first. And your temporall kingdome. And whiche of these .ij. kingdomes (suppose ye) is like to ouergrowe the other? ye, to put the other clere out of memory? Truely the kingdome of the bloudsuppers; for to theym [*But what avails it? They have since got more land than any Duke has.*] [*The kingdom is divided, and they have the overgrowing share:*]

¹ There is a custome in the Cytye, ones a yeare to haue a quest called the *warnmall queste*, to redress vices ; but alasse, to what purpose cometh it, as it is vsed ? If a pore man kepe a whore besides hys wife, & a pore mans wyfe play the harlot, they are punished, as well worthie. But let an alderman, a Ientleman, or a riche man, kepe whore or whores, what punishment is there ? Alasse, this matter is to bad.—*The Lamentacyon of a Christen against the Citye of London* (by Henry Brinklow, A.D. 1542), ed. 1548, sign. b. vii. back.

Quest or *Quest Men*, Persons who are chosen yearly in every Ward, and meet about *Christmas*, to enquire into Abuses and Misdemeanours committed therein, especially such as relate to Weights and Measures.—*Kersey's Phillips*, ed. 1706.

is giuen daily out of your kingdome. And that that is ones gyuen theim, comith neuer from theim agein. Suche lawes haue they, that none of theim may nether gyue nor sell nothing.

They will break any law, and will swallow all your substance.

Whate lawe can be made so stronge ageinst theim that they, other with money, or elles with other policy, will not breake and set at nought? whate kingdome can endure, that euer gyuith thus from him, and receyueth nothing agein? O, howe all the substaunce of your Realme forthwith, your swerde, power, crowne, dignite, and obedience of your people, rynneth hedlong ynto the insaciabill whyrlepole of these gredi goulafres,[1] to be swalowed and devoured!

They profess to pray for us and deliver us from purgatory,

¶ Nether haue they eny other coloure to gather these yerely exaccions ynto theyre hondes, but that they sey they pray for vs to God, to delyuer our soules out of the paynes of purgatori; without whose prayer, they sey, or at lest without the popes pardon, we coude neuer be deliuered thens; whiche, if it be true, then is it good reason that we gyue theim all these thinges, all were it C times as moche. But there be many men of greate litterature and iudgement that, for the love they haue vnto the trouth and vnto the comen welth, haue not feared to put theim silf ynto the greatest infamie that may be, in abiection of all the world, ye, yn perill of deth, to declare theyre oppinion in this mather, whiche is, that there is no purgatory, but that it is a thing inuented by the couitousnesse of the spiritualtie, onely to translate all kingdomes from other princes vnto theim, and that there is not one word spoken of hit in al holy scripture. They sey also, that if there were a purgatory, And also if that the pope with his pardons for money may deliuer one soule thens; he may deliuer him aswel without money: if he may

(which in many learned men's opinion exists not, but is their own invention;)

and if there be a purgatory, the Pope might deliver 1000 as well as one.

[1] Fr. *Goulfre, Gouffre:* m. A gulfe; whirlepoole, deepe hole, or vnmeasurable depth (of waters) that swallowes vp whatsoeuer approaches, or comes into, it.—*Cotgrave.*

A SUPPLICACYON FOR THE BEGGERS.

deliuer one, he may deliuer a thousand.: yf he may deliuer a thousand, he may deliuer theim all, and so destroy purgatory. And then is he a cruell tyraunt without all charite, if he kepe theim there in pryson and in paine, till men will giue him money. ¶ Lyke wyse saie they of all the hole sort of the spiritueltie, that if they will not pray for no man but for theim that gyue theim money, they are tyrauntes, and lakke charite, and suffer those soules to be punisshed and payned vncheritably, for lacke of theyre prayers. These sort of folkes they call heretikes, these they burne, these they rage ageinst, put to open shame, and make theim bere fagottes. But whether they be heretikes or no, well I wote that this purgatory, and the Popes pardons, is all the cause of translacion of your kingdome so fast into their hondes ; wherfore it is manifest it can not be of christ, for he gaue more to the temporall kingdome, he hym silfe paid tribute to Cesar, he toke nothing from hym, but taught that the highe powers shuld be alweys obeid : ye, he him silf (although he were most fre lorde of all, and innocent,) was obedient vnto the highe powers vnto deth. This is the great scabbe why they will not let the newe testament go a-brode yn your moder tong, lest men shulde espie that they, by theyre cloked ypochrisi, do translate thus fast your kingdome into theyre hondes, that they are not obedient vnto your highe power, that they are cruell, vnclene, vnmerciful, and ypochrites, that thei seke not the honour of Christ, but their owne, that remission of sinnes are not giuen by the popes pardon, but by Christ, for the sure feith and trust that we haue in him. Here may your grace well perceyue that, except ye suffer theyre ypocrisie to be disclosed, all is like to runne ynto theire hondes ; and as long as it is couered, so long shall it seme to euery man to be a greate ympiete not to gyue theim. For this I am sure

Margin notes: Again, they pray only for those who give them money. They who cannot pay, are called heretics, and are burnt. Christ, on the contrary, upheld powers, and paid tribute, which is their reason for withholding the New Testament in the mother tongue; for they seek their own honour, not Christ's.

12   THE PRIESTS DRAG CIVIL CAUSES INTO THEIR COURTS.

All are of my opinion, Lords, Knights, and yeomen; else the statute of mortmain robs us of salvation.

your grace thinketh, (as the truth is,) I am as good a man as my father, whye may I not aswell gyue theim as moche as my father did? And of this mynd I am sure are all the loordes, knightes, squire, gentilmen, and yemen in englond ; ye, and vntill it be disclosed, all your people will thinke that your statute of mortmayne was never made with no good conscience, seing that it taketh awey the liberte of your people, in that they may not as laufully by theire soules out of purgatory by gyuing to the spiritualte, as their predecessours did in tymes passed.

Declare, then, their hypocrisy.

¶ Wherfore, if ye will eschewe the ruyne of your crowne and dignite, let theire ypocrisye be vttered ; and that shalbe more spedfull in this mater then all the lawes that may be made, be they never so stronge. For to make a lawe for to punisshe eny offender, except it were more for to giue other men an ensample to beware to committe suche like offence, whate shuld yt avayle ?

Doctor Allen appealed to another Court to the derogation of your dignity;

Did not doctour Alyn, most presumptuously, nowe yn your tyme, ageynst all his allegiaunce, all that ever he coude, to pull from you the knowlege of suche plees as long vnto your hyghe courtes, vnto an other court, in derogacion of your crowne and dignite ?

and Doctor Horsey murdered Hunne, because he sued a writ of "premunire" against a priest.

Did not also doctor Horsey and his complices most heynously, as all the world knoweth, murdre in pryson that honest marchaunt Richard hunne? For that he sued your writ of premunire against a prest that wrongfully held him in ple in a spirituall court, for a mater wherof the knowlege belonged vnto your hyghe courtes. And whate punisshement was there done, that eny man

And one offender paid only £500 fin..:

may take example of to beware of lyke offence ? truely none, but that the one payd fiue hundreth poundes (as it is said) to the bildinge of your sterre chamber ; and when that payment was ones passed, the capteyns of his kingdome (bicause he faught so manfully ageynst your crowne and dignite,) haue heped to him benefice vpon benefice, so that he is rewarded tenne tymes as moche. The other (as it is seid) payde sixe hundreth poundes for him and his complices, whiche, forbicause that he had lyke wise faught so manfully ageynst your crowne and dignite, was ymmediatly (as he had opteyned your most gracyous pardon,) promoted by the capiteynes of his kingdome with benefice vpon benefice, to the value of .iiij. tymes as moche. who can take example of this punisshement to be ware of suche like offence? who is he of theyre kingdome that will not rather take courage to committe lyke offence, seyng the promocions that fill to this men for theyre so offending? So weke and blunt is your swerde to strike at one of the offenders of this croked and peruers generacyon.

marginalia: the other, £600; and each has received many times over what he was fined, from pluralities. Thus others will be encouraged to commit like offences, so weak is your power to strike the offenders.

¶ And this is by the reason that the chief instrument of your lawe, ye, the chief of your counsell, and he whiche hath youre swerde in his hond, to whome also all the other instrumentes are obedient, is alweys a spirituell man, whiche hath euer suche an inordinate loue vnto his owne kingdome, that he will mainteyn that, though all the temporall kingdoms and comonwelth of the worlde shulde therfore vtterly be vndone. Here leue we out the gretest mater of all, lest that we, declaring suche an horrible carayn of euyll ageinst the ministres of iniquite, shulde seme to declare the one onely faute, or rather the ignoraunce, of oure best beloued ministre of rightousnesse, whiche is, to be hid till he may be lerned by these small enormitees that we haue spoken of, to knowe it pleynly him silf. But whate remedy to releue vs your poore, sike, lame, and sore, bedemen? To make many hospitals for the relief of the poore people? Nay truely. The moo the worse; for euer the fatte of the hole foundacion hangeth on the prestes berdes. Dyuers of your noble predecessours,

marginalia: The reason is that your Chancellor is a priest, who loves only his own kingdom. Many hospitals will not help us, for the priests will get the best part, as they have done with your ancestors' gifts.

MAKE THE STURDY LOOBIES WORK.

kinges of this realme, haue gyuen londes to monasteries to giue a certein somme of money yerely to the poore people, wherof, for the aunciente of the tyme, they giue neuer one peny: They haue lyke wise giuen to them to haue a certeyn masses said daily for theim, wherof they sey neuer one. If the Abbot of westminster shulde sing euery day as many masses for his founders as he is bounde to do by his foundacion, .M. monkes were to fewe. wherfore, if your grace will bilde a sure hospitall that neuer shall faile to releue vs, all your poore bedemen, so take from theim all these thynges. Set these sturdy lobies a brode in the world, to get theim wiues of theire owne, to get theire liuing with their laboure in the swete of theire faces, according to the commaundement of god, Gene. iij. to gyue other idell people, by theire example, occasion to go to laboure. Tye these holy idell theues to the cartes, to be whipped naked about euery market towne til they will fall to laboure, that they, by theyre importunate begging, take not awey the almesse that the good christen people wolde giue vnto vs sore, impotent, miserable people, your bedemen. Then shall, aswell the nombre of oure forsaid monstruous sort, as of the baudes, hores, theues, and idell people, decreace. Then shall these great yerely exaccions cease. Then shall not youre swerde, power, crowne, dignite, and obedience of your people, be translated from you. Then shall you haue full odedience of your people. Then shall the idell people be set to worke. Then shall matrimony be moche better kept. Then shal the generation of your people be encreased. Then shall your comons encrease in richesse. Then shall the gospell be preached. Then shall none begge oure almesse from vs. Then shal we haue ynough, and more then shall suffice vs; whiche shall be the best hospitall that euer was founded for vs. Then shall we daily pray to god for your most noble estate long to endure.[1] *and all will ever pray for your long reign.*

Domins caluum fac regem.

[1] Sir Frauncys Bygod, about 1534, in his *Treatyse concernynge impropriations of benefices* thus supports the last remedy of the *Beggers Supplicacyon:*

But & as man might (sauyng their pacyence) be so bolde with them / what mater were it (vnder correction I speke) if all these improfytable sectes / and stronge sturdye route of idle paunches were a lytell poorer / to thende that the trew relygion of christ might thereby somthynge be sette vp and avaunsed / and syffycient company of the ministers of goddes true worde prouyded for in all partes. I praye you / what an idle sorte be founde and brought vp in Abbeyes / that neuer wyll laboure whyles they ben there / nor yet whan they come thence to other mens seruyce / in so moche that there goth a comen prouerbe: That he which hath ones ben in an abbey, wyll euer more after be slouthefull / for the whiche cause they ben called of many men / Abbey loutes or lubbers. And some saye that many of our holye fathers spende nat a lytell vpon my cosyn Iane / Elsabeth and Marget (ye knowe what I meane) insomoche that / *that* euen they which be most popysshe of all / & knowe none other god almost than the gret drafsacke of Rome / can nat deny this to be trew. *Idle paunches should be poorer.* *Once in an Abbey, ever idle; Abbey louts or lubbers.* *Monks' women.*

Page 6. *Priests' immorality.* The women were occasionally to blame. In a story told by the author of the *Ménagier de Paris*, a young wife married to an old husband from whom she gets no solace, thus answers the question of whom she will love: "Mère, j'aimeray le chapellain de ceste ville, car prestres et religieux craingnent honte, et sont plus secrets. Je ne vouldroie jamais amer un chevalier, car il se vanteroit plus tost, et gaberoit de moy, et me demanderoit mes gages* à engager." Compare Robert of Brunne's complaint in his *Handlyng Synne* of these women who *will* have priests. But the lechery of the monks, &c., is continually complained of throughout Early English Literature; see the series of extracts on this subject in my *Ballads from Manuscripts*, p. 59—86 (Ballad Soc. 1868), and *The Image of Ypocresye*, ib. p. 194-5, &c.

Page 6. *Check to the increase of Population by the not-marrying of the Clergy.* This is complained of in the Record-Office MS Dialogue between Cardinal Pole and Lupton, written by Starkey, one of Henry VIII's chaplains, which Prof. Brewer has recommended us to print, and which we have had copied. Lupton is made to say: "I haue thought long & many a day a grete let to the increse of chrystun pepul, the law of chastyte ordeynyd by the church, whych byndyth so gret a multytude of men to lyue theraftur, as, al secular prestys, monkys, frerrys, channonys, & nunnys, of the wych, as you know, ther ys no smal nombur; by the reson wherof the generatyon of man ys maruelously let & mynyschyd. Wherfor, except the ordynance of the church were, (to the wych I wold neuer gladly rebel,) I wold playnly Iuge that hyt schold be veray conuenyent somethyng to relese the band of thys law; specyally consyderyng the dyffyculty of that grete vertue, in a maner aboue

* Peut-être faudroit-il *bagues*, effets, joyaux.—J. Pichon.

nature..." Pole answers "... in this mater I thynke hyt were necessary to tempur thys law, *and*, at the lest, to gyue *and* admyt al secular pr*e*stys to mary at theyr lyberty, co*n*sydyryng now the grete multytude *and* nowmbur of them. but as touchyng mo*n*kys, chanonys, frerys, *and* nu*n*nys, I hold for a thyng veray co*n*uenyent *and* mete, in al wel-ordeynyd co*m*myn welys, to haue certayn monasterys *and* abbeys, to the wych al such as, aftur lauful proue of chastyte before had, may retyre, *and* from the besynes *and* vanyte of the world may wythdray themselfe, holly gyuyng theyr myndys to prayer, study, *and* bye co*n*templatyon. thys occasyon I wold not haue to be taken away from chrystyan pollycy, wych ys a grete comfort to many febul *and* very soulys, wych haue byn oppressyd wyth wordly vanyte. but as touchyng the secular prestys, I vtturly agre wyth you, *and* so that obstacul to take away, wych lettyth by many ways the increse of our pepul, as many other thyngys dow more also; among the wych a nother chefe, aftur my mynd, ys thys:—that grete multytude of s*e*ruyng men, wych in s*e*ruyce spend theyr lyfe, neu*er* fyndyng mean to marry co*n*uenyently, but lyue alway as co*m*myn corruptarys of chastyte."

Page 7. The good luck of a wench who is taken as a priest's concubine is noticed in the *Poem on the Evil Times of Edward II.* (Camden Soc. *Political Songs,* 1839 ; Percy Soc. 1849), "And wel is hire that first may swich a parsoun kacche in londe," *ib.* p. 62.

Pages 9 and 12. *Richard Hunne's case.* "In the year 1514, a citizen of London, named Richard Hunne, a merchant tailor, fell into a dispute with the parson of a country parish in Middlesex, about a gift of a bearing-sheet, which the clergyman demanded as a mortuary, in consequence of an infant child of Hunne's having died in his parish, where it had been sent to be nursed. Hunne made some objection to the legality of the demand; but it is probable that he was secretly inclined to the new doctrines, and that this was the true cause of his refusal. Being sued in the spiritual court by the parson, he took out a writ of premunire against his pursuer for bringing the king's subjects before a foreign jurisdiction, the spiritual court sitting under the authority of the pope's legate. This daring procedure of the London citizen threw the clergy into a fury, and, as the most effectual way of crushing him, recourse was had to the terrible charge of heresy, upon which Hunne was apprehended and consigned to close imprisonment in the Lollard's Tower at St Paul's. After a short time, being brought before Fitzjames, bishop of London, he was there interrogated respecting certain articles alleged against him, which imputed to him, in substance, that he had denied the obligation of paying tithes,—that he had read and spoken generally against bishops and priests, and in favour of heretics,—and lastly, that he had 'in his keeping divers English books prohibited and damned by the law, as the Apocalypse in English, epistles and gospels in English, Wycliffe's damnable works, and other books containing infinite errors, in the which he hath been long time accustomed to read, teach, and study daily.'[*] It appears that Hunne was frightened into a qualified admission of the truth of these charges; he confessed that although he had not said exactly what was asserted, yet he had 'unadvisedly spoken words somewhat sounding to the same; for the which,' he added, 'I am sorry, and ask God mercy, and submit me unto my Lord's charitable and favourable correction.' He ought upon this, according to the usual course, to have been enjoined penance and set at liberty; but, as he still persisted in his suit against the parson, he was the same day sent back to his prison, where, two days after, namely, on the 4th of December, he was found

[*] Foxe, p. 737.

suspended from a hook in the ceiling, and dead. The persons in charge of the prison gave out that he had hanged himself; but a coroner's inquest came to a different conclusion. According to the account in Burnet, the jury 'did acquit the dead body, and laid the murder on the officers that had the charge of that prison;' and, by other proofs, they found the bishop's sumner * and the bellringer guilty of it. It may be suspected that the excited feelings and strong prejudices of the coroner's jury had perhaps as much share as the weight of circumstantial evidence in winning them to the belief of this not very probable story; but, be that as it may, the violence and indecency shown on the other side were fully equal to any they can be thought to have displayed. While the inquest was still going on, the Bishop of London and his clergy began a new process of heresy *against Hunne's dead body*. The new charges alleged against Hunne were comprised in thirteen articles, the matter of which was collected from the prologue or preface by Wycliffe to the English Bible that had been found in his possession. He, or rather his dead body, was condemned of heresy by sentence of the Bishop of London, assisted by the Bishops of Durham and Lincoln, and by many doctors of divinity and the canon law; and the senseless carcase was actually, on the 20th of December, committed to the flames in Smithfield. This piece of barbarity, however, shocked instead of overawing the public sentiment. The affair now came before the parliament, and a bill, which had originated in the Commons, was passed, restoring to Hunne's children the goods of their father, which had been forfeited by his conviction. This, however, did not put an end to the contest. When the Bishop of London's chancellor and sumner had been charged on the finding of the coroner's jury as both principals in the murder, the convocation, in the hope probably of drawing off attention to another part of the case, called before them Dr Standish, who had asserted the claims of the civil power in a debate before the king, and put him upon his defence for what he had said on that occasion; and an appeal was made to the conscience of Henry, that he would not interpose to shield the delinquent from justice, as he regarded his coronation oath, and would himself escape the censures of holy church. Henry's headstrong and despotic character had scarcely yet begun to develop itself; his pride as a true son of the church had received no check from coming into collision with any of his other selfish and overmastering passions: when the convocation, therefore, assailed him in this manner on the one hand, and the parliament on the other likewise addressed him 'to maintain the temporal jurisdiction, according to his coronation oath, and to protect Standish from the malice of his enemies,' he was thrown into great perplexity. So, to free his conscience, he commanded all the judges, and the members both of his temporal and his spiritual councils, together with certain persons from both houses of parliament, to meet at Blackfriars, and to hear the matter argued. This was done accordingly; and the discussion was terminated by the unanimous declaration of the judges, that all those of the convocation who had awarded the citation against Standish had made themselves liable to a premunire. Soon after, the whole body of the lords spiritual and temporal, with all the judges and the king's council, and many members also of the House of Commons, having been called before the king at Baynard's Castle, Cardinal Wolsey, in the name of the clergy, humbly begged that the matter should be referred to the final decision of the pope at Rome. To this request, however, Henry made answer, with much spirit, ' By the permission and ordinance of God, we are king of England; and the kings

---

* Or summoner, the officer employed to cite parties before the ecclesiastical courts, more commonly called the apparitor.

of England in times past had never any superior, but God only. Therefore, know you well that we will maintain the right of our crown, and of our temporal jurisdiction, as well in this as in all other points, in as ample a manner as any of our progenitors have done before our time.' The renewed solicitations of the Archbishop of Canterbury, that the matter might at least be respited till a communication could be had with the court of Rome, had no effect in moving the king from his resolution ; and Dr Horsey, the Bishop of London's chancellor, against whom warrants were out, on the finding of the inquest, for his trial as one of the murderers of Hunne, seemed to be left to his fate. At this point, however, the clergy, or perhaps both parties, saw fit to make advances towards an accommodation : it was agreed that Horsey should surrender to take his trial; that he should not stand upon his benefit of clergy, but plead not guilty : and that, satisfied with this concession, the attorney-general should admit the plea, and the prisoner be discharged. This form was gone through, and Horsey immediately left London, where, it is said, he never again showed his face. Dr Standish, however, was also, by the king's command, dismissed from his place in the court of convocation, so that the issue of the business by no means went altogether against the clergy. But, besides the augmented popular odium to which they were exposed, from the strong suspicion that was entertained that Hunne had been murdered, a heavy blow had been undoubtedly dealt at their favourite pretension of exemption from the jurisdiction of the civil courts in criminal cases."—*Macfarlane' Cab. Hist. of England*, vol. vi., p. 113—116.

Page 12. *Doctor Alyn.* By the sayd power Legantine, he [Wolsey] kept also generall visitations through the Realme, sending Doct. Iohn Alein, his Chaplein, riding in his gowne of Veluet, & with a great traine, to visite all religious houses.—*Foxe*, 1576, 3rd edit., p. 960.

Page 2. *The tenth part of euery seruauntes wages.* "Then the proving of testaments, the prizing of goods, the bishop of Canterbury's prerogative ; is that not much through the realm in a year? *There is no servant but that he shall pay somewhat of his wages.*"—Tyndale's *Obedience of a Christian Man*, Parker Soc.'s edit. of Tyndale's "Works," vol. i. p. 237.

A Supplycacion

to our moste Soueraigne Lorde Kynge Henry the Eyght /, Kynge of England, of Fraunce, and of Irelande /, & moste ernest Defender of Christes Gospell /: Supreme Heade vnder God here in Erthe /, next & immedyatly of his Churches of Englande and Irelande.

Matthei .ix.

The harveste is greate, but the laborers are fewe. Wherfore praye the lorde of the harveste to sende forthe laborers into his harveste.

A Supplication to our moste Soueraigne Lorde Kynge Henry the Eyght, Kynge of England /, of Fraunce /, and of Irelande, &c.

[1] M Ost dreade Soueraigne Lorde & most Christen Prynce, / when I remembre the lamentable & wonderfull great blyndnes wherin the most parte of all Englande, not onely of the layete, called the temporaltie /, but also of the clergie, / haue pytuously erred and wandered many hundereth yeres /, acceptinge /, reputynge /, & most vngodly, / erronyousely /, and blyndely /, estemynge the bysshop of Rome to be supreame head ouer & aboue all Christen congregations; and in dyuerse other poyntes suche as be touchynge the necessarye articles of our faithe; I coulde not but meruell how, and by what meanes, suche pestilent errours and horrible darke blyndenes coulde, or myght, entre /, invade, & ouerflowe this your realme /, & to contynewe so longe in the same /, not espied /, perceyued /, nor repelled. Consideringe, that by all that tyme and space, this your realme (as the most parte of men dyd then iudge and esteame) was well endowed /, replenyshed /, and furnyshed with many profounde lerned clerkes /, wherof some were bysshops, archedeacons /, deanes /, prebendaries /, parsons /, doctours /, bachelars in deuinite /, & other profounde

Marginal notes: When I remember the blindness in which the clergy and laity of England have wandered many hundred years, I can but marvel why such errors have been allowed to continue. Considering the number of learned men in this realm, clerks of both universities,

[1] A six-line ornamental initial letter in the original.

lerned clerkes in bothe t*h*e Vniuersytees, which were /
graue /, sage /, & auncyent fathers. Contemplatinge
and reuoluinge these things in my mynde—not a lytle
moued /, troubled /, and vexed with t*h*e same /—I
applyed me wit*h* all my powre & dyligence, exquysytely
to serche & to knowe the originall grounde & cause
therof. And, in co*n*clusyon, amo*n*gest other things it
chau*n*ced me to reade in the .v. chapter of Ezay a pro-
position that muche lamenteth t*h*e captyuite and bondage which co*m*meth & groweth to all people for lacke
of knowleage in Godds Worde /; sayeng /, "Therfore
co*m*meth my flocke also into captyuite /, because they
haue not vnderstandinge /; their glory is famyshed
wit*h* hunger /, & their pryde marred wit*h* thyrste.
Therfore gapeth hell and openeth her mouthe meruel-
ously wyde." By this text, graciouse Lorde, it appeareth that all myserable blyndenes, captyuite, &
bondage vnder synne /, co*m*meth for lacke of knowleage
in Gods Worde. I had forgotten, at that tyme /, that
Christ reproued the Pharasees /, sayeng /, "You erre
not knowinge the Scriptures;" which reproue and rebuke shulde haue ben a suffycient admonycio*n* and
doctryne to me, and to all other; wherby we myght
haue knowen that all erroure commeth for lacke of
vnderstandinge & knowledge in the Scriptures. But
by what reason, then, coulde there be suche erroure and
blyndenes for lacke of knowleage in Gods Worde in
this your realme, most gracyouse Lorde /, seing there
were suche profounde clerkes, & auncyent fathers /,
bysshops, and studentes in the same /, which dyd
teache & preache vnto the people co*n*tynually? The
Apostle Paul, in the .vi. chapter to Timothe, descrybeth
two kyndes of doctrynes; / the one he calleth a godly
doctryne & a doctryne of helth /; the other he calleth
a proude doctrine, full of vnprofitable questions /,
stryuynge more for wordes than for godly knowleage /;

[margin notes: I tried to find out the cause of this blindness, and happening to read the fifth chapter of Isaiah, I found that lack of knowledge was the cause of all the harm. Mar. xij. I had forgotten that Christ said, "Ye do err, not knowing the Scriptures," which rebuke ought to have been sufficient. But how could there be error from not knowing the Scriptures? There are numbers of profound clerks and ancient fathers in the country who teach the people. But Paul says there are two kinds of knowledge, one a doctrine of health, the other unprofitable]

WANT OF KNOWLEDGE. 23

"wherof spryngeth envy /, stryffe /, raylings /, euyll surmysyngs /, & vayne dysputacions of men with corrupte myndes, destytute of the trueth /; which thinke that lucre is godlynes." This kynde of lernynge and subtle dysputacyons vnto this daye we call scole matters /; from the which Paul commaundeth all Christyans to separate them selues. Soche clerkes, sayeth Paul /, be "euer lernynge /, but neuer atteyne to the knowleage of the trueth." With suche wayne, vngodly, and vnprofitable lerninge /, this your realme, most redoubted Soueraigne, was ouer moche replenyshed through the preachinge and teachinge of suche scole men & subtyll disputers /; otherwise called deceyuers. Which was one of the causes of our myserable blyndnes /, and of dyuerse errours and abuses spronge vp and crept into this your Graces realme. For certeynely, if the clerkes, of this your Graces realme /, had bene endowed with true knowledge of Gods Worde /, and had also syncerely preached the same /, althoughe suche errours and blyndnes had entered into this realme /; yet they shulde neuer haue so longe contynewed in the same /, but we shulde haue bene delyuered through the Worde clerely from them. As Christe saieth: "If you continewe in my wordes /, then are you my very disciples /, & shall knowe the trueth /, & the trueth shall delyuer yow /, and make you free." Therfore, most dread Soueraigne Lorde /, seinge that all erroure /, spyrytuall blyndnes /, myserable captyuite /, and seruyle bondage vnto synne, commeth for lacke of knowledge and syncere vnderstandinge in the Holy Scriptures /; and, of the contrarye parte,/ through the knowleage & syncere vnderstandinge of the Holy Scripturs, we knowe God our Father and his Sonne, Ihesus Christ, our Lorde /, which is eternall liffe /; we be also become free from all condempnation of synne. And through the syncere and true know-

—from the latter we must separate ourselves. *ij. Ti. iij.*

There is too much vain, ungodly learning, and this comes of the preaching and teaching of the Schoolmen,

for which the clergy are to blame,

because they do not sincerely preach God's word.

Io. viij.

As all errors spring from a lack of knowledge of the Scriptures,

and through knowledge of them we know God, *Ioa. v. Io. xvij.*

leage of *the* Worde we be newly regenerate, & become *the* childerne of God /, the habitacle and dwellinge place of the Holy Ghoste /, which moueth & steareth vs euer to mortefye the fleshe /, & all her synfull lusts and concupiscence, / [and] to abhor and resyst vice. What is then so necessary, good, and profitable for the Christian people, bothe spirituall and cyuile wealthe /, as the Worde wherby we receyue faithe /, & by faithe, the Holy Ghoste? What troubleth all commen wealthes /, but treason /, murder, thefte /, couetousnes, / adulterye /, extorcion /, whordome, / dronckenes /, periurye /, & suche other synne? / as saythe the Holy Ghoste: "Iustice and rightuousnes maketh the people wealthy /; but synne maketh *the* people most myserable." And all these the faithfull, through *the* true and syncere vnderstandinge of Gods Worde /, doo euer studye and labour to ouercome /, and vtterly to abholyshe by faythe. As Paul sayeth: "They which be Christes /, doo crucyfye the fleshe, with her lustes and concupiscence." All good workes and counceyles [be] encreased and stablyshed through faythe. There is no study /, striffe /, nor laboure agaynst synne, but through faithe. All conscyences that be quyet from synnes /, onely through faythe be made quyet. As Paul sayeth /: "Because we are iustyfyed by faithe /, we are at peace with God, through our Lorde Ihesus Christ." What counforte hathe any Christian man in aduersytyes /, temptacions /, desperation /, but onely by fayth in Gods Worde? The Christyan man hathe noo refuge nor helpe to resyst synne /, but onely by Gods Worde /, as our Sauiour Christ dyd /; wherin he must fyxe a sure and constant faythe. Faythe causeth vs and all ours / to be acceptable in *the* syght of God. For a conclusion /: "What soeuer is not of fayth that same is synne." And withowte a constante and sure fayth /, it is impossyble to please God. All

FOR EVILS NOW PREVALENT.

men maye well perceyue / that, by the lawes, and by the iuste execution of them /, although synne may be for a tyme cohybyted and restrayned /, yet it can not be suppressed and abholyshed /, but onely through fayth. For there was neuer more godly lawes made for the punyshmente of synne /, nor neuer more iuste and godly executyon of lawes admynistred /; and yet there was neuer more synne raygnynge. For cyuyle lawes made by man / can not be of greater effycacye or strength /, nor worke greater perfectyon, vertue, and good wyll in man /, than the lawe of God: but the lawe of God not onely worketh no obedyence or vertue /; but rather, through occasyon taken of the infirmyte of the fleshe /, steareth vp synne, / as sayethe Paul: "I knowe not what luste dyd meane /, except the lawe had sayed, thow shalte not luste. But synne toke an occasyon by the meanes of the commandemente /, and wrought in me all maner of concupiscence:/ for verely, without the lawe, / synne was dead." "I ones," sayth Paul /, "lyued without lawe; but when the commandement came /, synne reuyued, / and I was dead /: and the very same commaundement, which was ordeyned vnto lyffe /, was founde to be vnto me an occasyon of deathe." But nowe, graciouse Lorde /, for asmoche as it appeareth / that the lawe of God was not geuen to take awaye synne /, but rather to declare and to punyshe synne; moche lesse any lawe made by man / can auoyde and put away synne. But faythe is the true instrument appoynted by God /, wherby synne is ouercome & exiled. As the Scripture sayeth /, that "God through faithe / dothe puryfye & make cleane all hartes." Also Christ sayethe /: "Nowe are yow cleane /, by the meanes of the wordes / whiche I haue spoken vnto you." This faythe shall cause /, noryshe, and breade / true obeydyence /, and all other vertues, in your Graces subiectes hartes /; wherby they shall be

Sin cannot be suppressed except through faith.

There never were more godly laws made, and laws never were better enforced than now; and yet there was never more sin.

God's law does not bring obedience, but rather stirs men up to sin, as St Paul says it did with him.

Ro. vij.

Ro. vij.

The Law of God was given, not to take away, but to punish, sin.

Act. xv.

Io. xv.

Faith will produce and nourish true obedience to the laws of God and man.

26 NEGLECT OF PREACHING.

enforced to laboure, not onely to obserue & kepe Godes lawes /, but also all your Graces ordynances, commaundementes, and lawes /, without grudge or murmuracyon. This faythe, as the Apostle sayeth, "commethe by hearinge" of Gods Worde preached /; wherof byshops, parsons /, vicars /, & suche other, called to haue spirituall cure /, be, or shulde be, dylygent mynisters /; to whose vocatyon iustely parteyneth to declare and publyshe Gods Worde, syncerely & truely, / to all the people commytted to their spirituall charge. Most myghty Prynce, wherfor, if the pastours appoynted to preache & teache Gods Worde /, within this your Graces realme, / doo not dyligently instructe & teache the people commytted to their spirituall charge with the sayd Worde, / accordinge as they be commaunded in the Scriptures, Act. xx., i. Pet. v., and Malache. ii.[1]; all kynde of synne shall increase and abounde, / & the people vtterly be devyded. As sayethe the Holy Ghoste: "When the worde of God is not preached, the people perysheth." Also the Wyse Man sayethe: "All men be vayne in whom there is not the knowleage of God." Wherfore, without any doubt, the wante and lacke of preaching of Godes Worde syncerely and truely hathe bene the very originall grounde and cause of all the insurrection, / commotion /, [and] dyscention /, which hathe rysen, or begone, within this your Graces realme, or any parte therof. For through the want of preachyng of Godes Worde synce[re]ly, haue entered in all popyshe blyndenes /, vayne & dead ceremonyes /; mennes tradycyons be crept into the conscyences of the symple innocentes, in the steade of the lawe of God. Yea, ydolatrye, and all hypocrysye, with detestable superstycyon, for lacke of the lyght of Godes Worde /, is become Gods seruyce. And yet, notwithstandinge this wante & lack of knowleage in Godes Worde & the

Rom. x.
And of this faith the clergy should be ministers;

because it is their duty to teach it to the people sincerely and truly.

If they do not, sin will abound, and the people become divided, and perish.
Act. xx.
i. Pe. v.
Mal. ij.

Proue. xxix.
Sa. xiij.

The want of preaching has caused insurrections and commotions in the realm;

brought in popish blindness, vain ceremonies, men's traditions,

idolatry, and hypocrisy: and all for lack of a knowledge of the Bible.

---

[1] Orig. .xx.

euyll which commethe manyfestly therof /, (the more it is to be lamented /) there be many popishe monckes, which late were abbottes, (to whom not onely vnworthely /, but also vniustely /, were geven greate pensyons) and many of their covent monckes, hauinge nother lernynge nor other godly qualytyes, (apte, meate, or convenyent to be in spirituall pastours) be nowe admytted to haue cure of soules. And some suche which ded neuer knowe what is a soule /, nor yet be able to haue cure ouer one soule, / be nowe admytted to haue charge ouer an hundreth and many moo /, to the increase of all yngnorancye, and all popishe blyndnes /; the hyghe waye & meanes to let in all kynde of synne, / to the vtter dampnacion of all the soules commytted to their spirituall charge. Alas! doo nother the patrones of suche benefyces /, nor yet the incumbentes, ponder, or regarde, Gods threatenyngs by his prophete Ezechiell, sayeng: / "As truely as I lyue, sayeth the Lorde, for asmuche as my shepe are robbed, and deuowred of the wilde beastes of the felde, hauynge noo shepeherde, / and seing that my shepherdes take noo regarde of my shepe /, but feade them selues onely, / and not my shepe: Therfore, here the worde of the Lorde, O ye shepherdes: / thus sayeth the Lorde God, Beholde, I my selfe will [be] vpon the shepherdes /, and requyre my shepe from their handes /, and make them cease from feadinge of my shepe; yea, the shepherdes shall feade them selues nomore: / for I will delyuer my shepe owte of their mowthes /, so that they shall not deuoure them after this." If this threatenynge be not suffycient warnynge & monycion to suche blynde shepherdes /, yet, at the lest, let them feare Goddes curse pronownced in the same chapiter agaynst suche neglygent and ingnorant shepherdes; / sayenge: "Woo be to the shepherdes of Israell that feade them selues! /

Many monks are admitted to the cure of souls,

having neither learning nor godly qualities;

some of them never knew what a soul is, and certainly were never able to have cure of souls. This increases ignorance and sin, and leads to the damnation of the souls committed to their charge.

Patrons and incumbents do not regard God's threatenings Ezech. xxxiiij.[1]

by Ezekiel, against such as rob His sheep to feed themselves.

He will require His sheep at their hands.

If they do not regard this threatening, at least let them fear the curse pronounced by the same prophet, who says:— "Woe to the shepherds who feed themselves!

---

[1] Orig. xiiij.

shulde not the shepherdes feade the flocke /? yow haue eaten vp the fatt, / yow haue clothed yow with the wolle /, the best fedd haue youe slayne /: but the flocke haue yow not noryshed /." Heauen and erthe shall muche rather perishe /, than these wordes, wherwith God threatened suche pastours, shalbe found vntrue /; that is /, "I will requyre my flocke of the handes of the shepherde." Suerly, most myghty Prynce, it is to busye an office /, to muche and laborouse, for one spirituall shepherde, (althoughe he were very expert and connynge) to guyde, ordre /, and kepe /, two or thre flockes of shepe /, specially beyng so farre dystant one from an other /, that the sayd shepherde can not be dayly present with them /, to se the governaunce of them /, whose nature is dayly to falle into dyuerse offences and spirituall dyseases. For the office of a good shepherd is, not onely to feade his shepe in good pasture /, but also to seke the lost shepe /, to call agayne the strayed shepe in-to the ryght waye /, to salue and to make hole the broken which is broken by aduersyte /, the weake and sycke shepe in the faythe /, with the counfortable promyses of God /, declared in the Gospell /, to make stronge & constant; and, in conclusyon, to aduenture his liffe (if nede requyre) for the defence of his shepe /. Ever circumspecte, lyeng in wayte / to resyst the roringe lyon /, whiche neuer slepeth /, "goinge abowte and seakynge whome he maye devoure." Suche, I saye, shulde be their diligence and dayly cure over their flocke shewed /, that, not onely their shepe /, but also all other /, seing and perceyvinge[1] their greate paynes and labours sustayned and taken for the helpe and counforte of their shepe /, the gentle entertayninge with all pacyence /, humylyte, & meakenes /; the fatherly love /, cure /, and affeccion, which the said byshops and other pastours shulde

---

[1] Orig. scing and preceyvinge.

daylye shewe /, exercyse, & practyse towardes Christes flocke, commytted to their spirituall charge; shall iudge them, not onely good shepherdes, which enter in by the dore, / but also shall receyue & take them to be most gentle /, prouydent, kynde, / & lovinge spirituall fathers. But, most prudent Gouernoure, how shall this fatherly cure /, love /, zeale /, & affection /, be shewed by the pastoure to his spirituall shepe, which daylye cowcheth and wayteth in your Graces housholde and courte /, and in other noble & worshipfull mennes howses /, attendinge to please men whych is called onely to serue God? And, not withstandinge his callinge to be a shepherde to feade Christes flocke, / yet he will scase se and visyte them ones in the yere. And when he visyteth his shepe /, what ghostely councell he geveth them /, God knoweth. But, for the more parte /, he loketh more to his owne profett than to their wealthe. Alas! the ambicyouse appetyte & burnynge covetuouse desyre of the yerely commodyties /, profettes, and advauntages of the benefyces /, hathe vtterly extynguyshed and supped vp the spirituall love /, zeale, and affeccion which ought to be in the spirituall shepherdes. So that nowe it is straunge and wonderfull to se, or knowe, one iustely to execute his offyce. Is this the honowre of any kynge, or of any other gouernowre /, that, vnder the cloke and coloure of hys seruyce /, a byshope or pryste, called to feade the flocke of Christe /, shall leaue the same vntaught /, and so transgresse the commaundement of Christe for the pleasure of men? Haue not kynges and other rulers sufficyent to endowe their chapelaynes /, without retayninge suche which haue receyued lyuinge and stypende to be in their churches feadinge Christes flock? This is tomoche dishonoure to the higher powers /, agaynste Goddes commaundement & word, to retayne an other mans seruaunt. But certenly althoughe

The non-resident shepherd cannot show these virtues;

he does not visit his flock above once a year, and when he does what counsel he gives them, God knows.

It is wonderful to find one shepherd who does his duty.

Should a king so transgress for the pleasure of men?

Kings and rulers keep chaplains who have other livings,

which is a great dishonour to the commands of God.

your Highnes, or other rulers, wolde nother call nor retayne suche ambyciouse blynde guydes and couetouse pastours /, yet they their selfe will, by their fryndes, make importunate sute, and laboure to be in seruice with youre Magestye, and with other rulers. The cause is thys / (one inconuenyence graunted /, many folowe): there is a lawe made in this your noble realme /, that all spirituall parsons of youre counsell maye haue thre benefyces with cure. And all the chaplaynes of the Kynge, / Quene /, prynce /, prynces, or of any of the Kyngs children /, brethren, / sisters /, vncles and auntes /, maye haue lycence to haue two benefyces with cure. Euery duke /, marques /, erle /, vycounte /, archebysshope /, bysshope /, with dyuers other estates, aswell men as women, maye haue two chaplaynes which maye haue two benefyces with cure /. And also dyuerse other degres of scole maye haue euery one two benefyces with cure /; so that ouer one of his cures, althoughe he take the profyttes, yet from that he muste neades be no[n] resydent; and, peraduenture, to bothe he wilbe no feader nor teacher. And also, in the same estatute, all attendaunce in the courte and all other attendaunces vpon suche noble and worshipfull men which be lycenced to haue chaplaynes, maye be not resydent; / yea, pylgrymes, in the tyme of goynge and commynge from their pylgrymage, be by that estatute dyspenced to be non resydent. O Lorde, where was the light of thy worde /, which shulde haue bene written in the hartes of the makers of that estatute? If there had ben godly shepherdes, which had dyligently executyd their office and callynge /, we had neuer wandered so blyndely to agree or consent to the makynge of any suche estatute. Doo we, which thinke vs Christen men, esteame spirituall benefyces to be nothinge els but lyvinges to be geuen at owre pleasure to prystes for seruyce done? Is not the benefyce geuen

in respecte of a spirituall offyce to be executyd & done? <small>livings to be given at pleasure?</small>
Doth not God commaunde straytely shepherdes to <small>God commands shepherds to feed their flocks,</small> feade their flocke dyligently? Can man, or any lawe made by man, dyspence with Gods commaundement? <small>and man's law cannot dispense with God's.</small> O Lorde, in thy handes be the hartes of all kynges and other rulers /; enlyghten theyr hartes, Lorde, with the light of thy worde, that they maye knowe and see this pestylent yll blyndenes /, which so longe hathe caused thy shepe to wander in darckenes. And, when they perceyue it, they maye haue grace and tyme to reforme the same, to thy glory and the helpe of this realme. And I shall euer desyer of God, and wishe in <small>I desire that patrons present only such to any temporal or spiritual office as are well known to them</small> my harte, to all suche as be called to be attendaunte nere youre Magestie, and all other gouernowres /, that for any carnall loue /, fauoure /, or affectyon whiche they beare to any man for kyndred /, frendshipe /, luker /, or otherwise /, they doo not make any suche vngodly suytes, petycions, or requestes to your Highnes, or to any other gouernowre, for any parson to be admytted to any offyce, other spirituall or temporall /, whome they doo not certeynly knowe, by most certeyne and sure proues and witnesses /, to be apte /, meate /, <small>to be fit for the duties required,</small> and conuenyent, aswell in lernynge as in condycions /, to excercise, vse, and to occupye suche offyce and rome /, wherunto he, by suche their sute m[ade], / shulde be called /, appoynted, and admy[tte]d (not onely for the shame, rebuke, and troble whiche, vpon dewe examynacion had, and founde contrary to their vntrewe sute) myght come and growe to them /; but also for the euyll <small>because of the mischiefs which may arise from such wrong appointments.</small> incommodyte and pestilent myschef which shall ensewe to all suche which shalbe commytted to his or their gouernaunce & charge. Alas, that euer amongest the <small>Alas, that the most godly office should become one of honour and lordly dignity,</small> Chrysten flocke, shulde be knowen or sene that suche office, which in Christes churche shulde be the most godly /, most necessary /, most spirituall, and most profytable, bothe to the bodye and sowle /, nowe is become

a worldely honowre /, a lordely dygnyte, / a riche, carnall, prowde lyuinge, estate, and countenance /; and the possessor therof, hauinge onely the name of a spirituall minyster /, but no vertue nor godly qualyte, which of right ought to be in euery suche minister. If this be well pondered and remembred, most mercyfull Gouernowre, / it is most to be lamented. But seynge this blyndnes hathe so longe contynewed, & somoch ewill hathe ensewed & folowed therof, in the defaulte of godly pastours[1] /; it is not onely nedefull aboue all thinges to be circumspect in chosynge ernestly tryed /, experte /, and well lerned ministers to preache Gods worde syncerely /, but also to compell the same to be demurante, abydinge, and resydent vpon their cures. And all suche whiche be crepte into benefices for luker & aduauntage, vpon vntrewe suggestion and false fayned sutes made, / which can not or doo not feade their flocke /, to depryue them of suche benefyces, because they other can not or doo not execute the offyce to that belonginge. Suerly no wyse man lyghteth a candell and putteth hym vnder a bushell. And if he set vp a candell (which, other for lacke of talowe or for other cause, can not geue light) shortely he taketh hym downe and putethe an other which can geue good light in his place. So all godly wyse men will order all spirituall lightes, which in dede can not geue godly lighte for lacke of spirituall grace which shulde be in them. For byshops and other pastors, which be chosyne & instytuted contrary to the ordynaunce appoynted & prescribed by Gods Worde /, which other doo not or can not execute the offyce perteyninge to his or their callynge /, be not godly & trewe byshops, but rather images & idolles, hauinge and bearinge onely the name and outwarde apparance of a byshoppe or pastor. But as concernynge the lernynge, vertue, &

[1] Orig. postours.

other godly qualyties whiche parteyne & be of greate necessyte and iustyce requysyte to be in euery godly pastor, / they haue nothinge lesse. For if Christ (which sayed to Peter " from henceforthe I make the a fysher to catche men ") doo not endowe the offycer wyth lernynge /, grace, / power, & good will to preache his worde, before patrons present hym to any suche spirituall office ; / the electe and admytted, notwithstandinge the admyssion and patrons presentment, / shall contynually abyde and remayne an hypocryte /: and suche one, which dothe not enter in by the dore /, but presumeth to enter withowte a weddynge garment, / whom Christ condempneth to owtwarde darckenes /, and also callethe hym a thef /, whose rewarde, withowte doubt /, shalbe, at the daye of the laste iudgement, with thefes /; if he repent not, and reasygne vp hys offyce, which he can not execute, fulfyll, and performe. Wherfore I mystruste not but that all suche which haue power to present and to admytte theyr clerkes to spirituall offyces, readynge this lytle boke for the dyscharge of theyr conscyence, and for the glory of God /, the commodyte and vtylite of the common wealthe (which will ensewe the godly presentacyon and admyssion of well lerned /, approued, & godly clerckes to spirituall offyces) will, from thenceforthe, applye and conforme them to the forme and maner of electyon of spirituall mynisters appoynted, prescrybed, and lymytted by Godes Worde /, which is this :—That euery man chosyn to vse any spyrituall offyce /, shulde be fyrste well proued, aswell for theyr lernynge as also for theyr other vertuouse condycions. Fyrst for theyr lernynge, wherwith they muste not onely be able to enstructe and teache the people commytted to theyr spyrytuall charge /, but also able to reproue other which resyst the same doctrine /, with many other godly qualyties. As it apperethe in the fyrste Epistle

and have none of the godly qualities requisite. If Christ do not endue him with learning and power to preach before he be admitted,

he shall be considered a hypocrite.

Ioan. x. Math. xxij. Such a one enters not in by the door, is without the wedding garment, and shall be condemned at the last.

Patrons, after reading this book, for the discharge of their conscience, and the good of the commonwealth,

ought only admit to livings according to God's Word,

which is this, that every man shall be first well proved in learning and virtue.

of Paul to Tymothe and also to Tyte. Nowe, moste myghty Defender of the Christyan religyon /, seinge that Godds Worde hathe prescrybed and declared that euery man, which shalbe called and appoynted to be a spyrituall mynister, muste fyrste be proued and knowen howe godly and spirytually he hathe enstructe and teached the people /; what lernynge he hathe in the Scriptures /, and not in the lawes /, to reproue errours and to condempne heresyes; what paynes he hathe taken in preachynge Godds Worde /; and also whether he hathe geuen good example of lyuinge accordinge to his doctryne. In this maner euery Christian ought to proue his clerke before he other present or admytt hym. But nowe also, moste benyngne Lorde /, consydre of the contrary parte, & remembre for what causes the kynges, your noble progenitors in tymes paste, haue chosen bysshopps /, & other patrons haue presented theyr clerckes to personagyes & vicaragyes to haue cure of sowles. These bothe causes well consydered, no man wyll greately meruell that we haue wandered so longe in blyndenes. For, in tymes paste, kynges haue geuen theyr bysshoprycks to theyr councellers / chaplaynes, whiche haue bene daylye attendauntes in the courte /; which also haue done to them good seruice / as enbasadoures /; or to suche which haue taken paynes in theyr householde /, as amners & deanes of the chappell /, clerks of theyr closett, & suche other officers /; where Gods Worde dothe not approue any byshopricke to be geuen to any man for any suche seruice done /, or for any suche paynes taken /; but onely for the gifte whiche he hathe from God to preache his worde /, & for the paynes & laboures susteyned in preachinge of the sayd worde. And as kynges, in tymes paste, haue abused their giftes of byshoprikes /, so noble men & worshipfull men, aswell of the clergie as of the layete, haue abused their presentacions to their prebendes, personages, & vicarages /; geuing them to their chaplaynes /, or to other, for kyndred in bloude, or for alyaunce; / or els to suche as haue ben surueyours of thier landes, / receyuoures of their rentes /, stuardes of their housholde /, faconers /, gardyners, or to suche other whom they fauoure for suche worldely seruice & qualyties. To suche they geue their benefyces as rewardes or wagies to hyrelynges, for suche seruice done /, or to be done /; hauinge lytle or noo regarde to the great charge and spirituall cure which, by Goddes Worde, belongeth to all suche spirituall offices. For kynges and rulers, in tymes paste, had noo lesse knowleage of any thynge / then of Godes Worde, which the subtyll byshops & crafty prystes were euer studiouse and desyrouse to kepe secrete from the hygher powers. For so longe as Godes Worde was kepte secrete and hyden from gouernours /, so longe the clergye dyd leade, not onely the kynges /, but also, all gouernowres & the commons, whyther they wolde. Thys was the crafty polycye of the clergye /, to kepe the knowlege of Gods Worde from all men /, that they myght vnlawfully and vnworthely be promoted to spirituall cures / and vse the profettes of them vngodly /; and that they myght also contynually exercyse their lustes and iniquyties. As Paul saythe: "They be agaynste all men; forbyddinge vs to speake to the people wherby they myght be saued /, that they myght fulfyll their iniquyte and synne contynually." Haue not some of the byshops, with their retynewe, at this daye practysed their olde polycy to extinguyshe the light through all Englande /, that they myght ones agayne leade vs quyetly in darckenes? Is not there a lawe made, through their crafte & subtylte, which geueth power to certayne commyssioners, wherof the byshoppes chaunceler or commyssarye shalbe named to be two of the commyssioners /, which shall haue full power to take

and have presented livings to surveyors, receivers of rents, falconers, gardeners, and such like, as wages to hirelings, or as rewards.

Kings and rulers were ignorant of God's Word in times past; the bishops were ever anxious to keep it secret.

This was the policy of the clergy to keep this knowledge from all men in order that they might be promoted to spiritual cures.

[i.] *The. ij.*

A law is made through their craft appointing commissioners

into their custodye all suche bokes wherin is conteyned any clause or artycle repugnaunte to any of the Syx Artycles, / and the same bokes to burne and dystroye, as to the discretion of thre of them shalbe thoughte expedyent? Marke well what they purpose by this estatute. Are there any bokes which write agaynste the Popes prymacie /, but they also write agaynste some of the Syx Artycles? Their coloure is to take awaye all bookes which wryte agaynste the Syx Artycles /; but their very intente, purpose, and meanyng is to take awaye all bookes, whiche conteyne any godly lernynge, that write agaynste the Byshop of Romes prymacy. Howe cruelly doo the byshops punyshe all them which pretende to haue lernynge, and specially in Godds Worde? Suche they call heretyques, and persecute with puttynge them to open shame /, with enprysonmente /, and, in conclusyon, with deathe most fearefull and paynefull. All this they doo to dyscorage all men from the studye of Gods Worde / fearinge leaste that, by suche studiouse braynes which learne Gods Worde and publyshe the same, their iniquyte shulde be made manyfest. What studye and paynes they take to kepe the light from the people! But no man, which knowethe the Scriptures, will meruell of this their policye and crueltye. For Saynt Iohan declarethe their practyse playnely, sayenge: "He that doth euyll hateth the light" /; and why? because his workes, whiche be euill, shulde not be reproued by the light. And, for asmuche as oure byshops countenaunce of lyuinge /, their greate possessyons /, and lordely domynyons in them, agreeth with Godds Worde /, as deathe with lyffe /, God with the deuill /, light with darckenes /; therfore they hate the light which declarethe the same /, and studye to suppresse the same by all craft and polycye. And, seinge they can so craftely iuggle, and haue suche frendshipe and fauoure[1] to conuey /, [&] brynge to passe / that all bookes shall come into their handes vndre the coloure of the Syx Artycles /, it is to be feared that, shortely, they will, by lyke crafte, subtylte and frendshipe, procure the Byble in Englyshe to be taken from the layete /; & then we shalbe ledd in darckenes by our byshops and other blynde gydes, and not pastoures, at theyr pleasure and will /; whiche is the effecte of all theyr study, laboure, and purpose. Nowe, most valeaunt Defender of Christ /, it appearethe playnely howe many myseryes we be wrapte in /, through the vngodly electyon of suche as be admytted to haue spyrytuall cure and offyce to teache Godds Worde /; whiche not onely haue lytle lernynge /, but also they be enemyes to all men whiche can and doo preache Gods Worde sy[n]cerely and trewly, / because they lyue contrarye to the same /, as I haue before declared /. And this is the orygynall grownde and cause of the abundaunce and increase of darkenes and of synne /; as also of the longe contynuaunce of popishe blyndnes whiche hathe raigned in this realme so longe. Wherfore, yf the byshops, and other elected and appoynted to be shepherdes accordinge to theyr vocatyon and callinge /, be not fyrste knowen and well proued to haue suche knowleage & godly doctryne /, so that they can, & also doo, instantely & dyligently preache Gods Worde, whiche is the light expellinge all darckenes of synne /, then muste nedes synne encrease & abounde, without any restraynte or brydle. "For if the light whiche is amongest yow be darckenes /, howe muche shall the darkenes be!" Youre Grace and your cyuile power doo punnyshe synne /, when it is done and commytted /, accordinge to the iustyce of lawes /, as to your vocatyon & office of right belongethe to doo. But the office and dewtye of the pastor is to preache Goddes Worde /,

[1] Orig. fououre.

38   THE ADVANTAGES OF

disposed to commit sin;

wherby he shall conuert the hart of the synner /, whiche is willinge & dissposed to doo synne /, so that he shall not breake fourthe to doo synne in the acte /, which the cyuyle powre, for the example of other, by equyte and iustyce is bounde to punyshe. Therfore

so that, through him, there is lesse sin, the higher powers have less occasion to execute the justice of the law, and men's lives are preserved.

the dyligent executyon of the office of the pastoure shalbe the pryncipall meane and occasyon that lesse synne shalbe commytted; / and so the higher powers shall haue lesse occasyon to execute the extreame iustyce of lawes /, and, consequently, many mens lyues, whiche nowe for lacke of the knowleage of Godes Worde shuld be loste for commyttinge murder /, felonye /, and suche other offences, / shall then be preserued that they shall not commytte suche offences /, which the hygher powers, by the lawes of equyte & iustyce, be compelled to condempne and to punyshe with deathe.

Wherefore it appears the good order of the realm depends upon the ministers of religion.

Wherfore, the godly tranquyllyte, reste, and peace of all this your realme, soueraygne Lorde /, and the good order of the same, hangeth and resteth moche vpon the godly and dyligent executyon of the office of pastors and of the spirituall shepherds, dewly called and ad-

It behoves patrons to be very careful in the bestowal of their patronage.

mytted accordinge to Godes Worde. Therfore it behoueth the presenter of the clercke to a benefyce and cure of sowles, to be cyrcumspect and well ware what clerke he doth present /; and that he haue good knowleage, experience, and proue of his clercke before he

If they present unfit pastors, such as do not feed the flock committed to them, Ezech. xxxiij.

present hym. For, if a pastour doo not feade the flocke of Christe commytted to his charge /, the deathe of their sowles shalbe required of his handes. As the prophete Ezechiell sayeth in the .xxxiij. chapi.: And if the patron willingely /, other for kyndred /, fauoure /, frendshippe /, seruice, or money /, present a clerke which he knoweth not to be so lerned in Gods Worde /, that he be able to instructe and teache the people commytted to his charge, bothe with the lawe of God and

they consent to the death of souls,

withe the Gospell /, every suche patron consenteth to

the deathe & dampnacion of the sowles commytted to
the charge of suche vnlerned preste. And therfore *and will be punished with eternal pain.*
suche a patron shall also be punyshed with lyke
payne /; whiche is eternall /, as the Apostell sayeth: *Rom. i.*
"Not onely they that doo euill /, but also they whiche
consent therunto, shalbe punyshed with lyke payne."
What wyse man liuynge wolde hyer a shepherde to *What man would hire a shepherd who would not feed his sheep?*
gouerne hys beastly & worldly shepe, which nother
wolde nor coulde feade /, handle /, salue, nor ones see
his shepe commytted to his charge? Suche a wyse
shepherde wolde shortely make his masters profet come
to lytle aduauntage. Surely, a wyse man wolde chose *If a wise man were deceived by his friends' persuasion, yet he would soon discharge him from his service.*
no suche shepherde. And if he were deceyued through
the persuasyon of some of his frendes /, yet, when he
hathe proued that he hathe no connynge nor dyligence /,
he will shortely dyscharge hym of his cure and seruice.
Shall we be estemed Christen men whiche haue more
tender loue and affectyon to owre corruptyble profett /,
than we haue to the honowre of God & the eternall
wealthe of the immortall sowles of owre Christen
bretheren /, whom Gode commaundeth [vs] to loue as
owre selfe? Christ ded not commytt to Peter the cure *Io. xxi.*
and charge of his shepe, before he asked thryse of *Christ asked Peter whether he loued Him, before He committed His sheep to his charge;*
Peter whether he loued hym. As who shulde saye, I
wolde not commytt my best beloued ioywell and treasure vnto the /, vnlesse thowe loue me hartely. I
wolde wyshe that all gouernowres and rulers in this
case wolde take example and folowe Christ, whiche, *and patrons should follow this example.*
knowynge the good wyll of Peters harte /, yet as one
ingnorante therof, ded demaunde this question of Peter *He knew Peter's good will, but He asked the question to give example to all His faithful followers.*
before he ded commytt the cure of his flocke to hym /;
therby to geue example & common doctryne to all his
faythfull folowers, that they shulde haue suche tender
and feruent loue towardes the Christen sowles /, that
they wolde not commytt the gouernaunce and cure of
them to any man /, but vnto suche of whom they haue

proue & sure knowleage /, that, aswell by their preachinge & syncere teachinge of Gods Worde /, as also by their vertuouse lyuinge consonante to the same Worde, they had vnfaynedly a faythfull harty loue towardes Chrystes flocke. A blynde eye, which can not dyrecte and leade the bodye, is a blemyshe and a burden to the naturall bodye /, and noo commodyte. In lykewyse a man, chosen to be a spyrytuall pastour, which hathe not the knowleage and grace to preache the lawe and the Gospell /, is but a blynde eye, not able to dyrecte and leade the spyrytuall bodye. Wherfore, if any patron chose any suche ingnorante man to be a pastoure /, a spirituall eye and light to leade the spirituall sowles /; he not onely deceyueth them, but also, asmoche as lyeth in hym, kyllethe the bodye / and dothe greate iniurye to Christes bloode. Now it maye please yowre Highnes to note and marke what myschef and inconuenyence folowe the electyon and admyssion of an ingnorante pastour.[1] Fyrste, if an ingnorante byshope in Gods Worde be admytted /, he can not execute his office because he knoweth not the Scryptures whiche teacheth hym what shulde perteyne to his owne office. And as the byshop is ignorante in Godes Worde /, so he admytteth suche as be vnlerned in Gods Worde /; evyn suche as by noo possybylite can execute the office of their callinge; idle parsons /, vnhappy / dronckerdes /, swerers /, common players at all vnthryftye games /, in whom there is no chastyte, / noo humylyte /, iustyce /, nor temperance. For a conclusion, / suche they admytte in whom there is noo holynes /, godly doctryne /, nor good example of lyuinge. To suche they commytte the healthe of sowles /, the flocke of Christe, dearely bought with his bloode /; by suche ydle and wicked harlottes the enheritaunce of Christe is troden vnder fote. All euyll condycions, maners,

[1] Orig. postour.

and doctrynes by them be tawght /; so that in the
steade of Holy Scripture is crepte in the doctryne of
lyes /, all superstycions /, dead & vayne ceremonyes /,
and lycence to doo all kynde of synne. Some of the *Some of them teach that souls are relieved by the ringing of bells, painting of pillars, setting up candles;*
blynde ignorante prestes teache the people that God is
honowred /, and soules releued of their paynes, through
the rynginge of belles /, painting of postes /, and settynge vp tapers and candelles before the sayd postes /,
whom the blynde prestes doo bothe sence & spryncle
with holy water. An other sorte of blynde shauelings
teache the people to gett heuen with fastynge /; this *by fasting on this or that day,*
prescripte daye & that daye /, with trentalles and
masses of scala celi /; with forbearinge of bodely workes
& kepinge ydle holy dayes /. They preache muche *and keeping Holy Days. They say much holiness stands in holy oil, holy chrism, holy water, and such like, and in keeping church ales.*
holynes and Gods seruice to stande in their holy oyle /,
holy creame /, holy water /, holy asshes /, hallowed
bedes /, mumblynge of a numbre of psalmes in Laten /,
keapinge of church ales, in the whiche with leappynge, /
daunsynge /, and kyssyng, they maynteyne the profett
of their churche (to the honoure of God, as they both
saye and thyncke). And thus the blynde leadeth the *Thus the blind lead the blind, and both fall into the ditch.*
blynde /, that both fall hedlonge into the lake of
eternall brenninge fyer. What naturall harte is there
whiche will not lamente the misery /, yea the dampnacion, most certenly thretenede by Gods Worde vnto all
ingnorante, and neglygent bysshopps, and other spyrytuall shepherdes, which doo not dylygently execute
theyr offyce and vocation? What honest louinge harte
doth not bewayle the habundaunce of synne /, the
longe myserable blyndnes, wherin this realme hath
ben ledd and wrapped in through the yngnorancye and
neglygence of suche blynde guydes? But is there any *Such things make all Christians mourn when they remember the huge number of souls which are utterly damned.*
Chrysten harte which can forbere contynuall syghinge
and mornynge /, remembringe the multytude, yea, the
infynyte numbre, of sowles (whiche without the greate
mercye of God, passing all his worckes) through ing-

norancye & negligence of suche blynde shepherdes /, be vtterly cast awaye & dampned? What good cyuyle harte wolde not, I saye, lament and bewayle the greate burden wherwith this your realme (gracyouse Lorde) is ouercharged through the greate multytude of chauntery prestes /, soule prestes /, chanons /, resydensaryes in chathedrall churches /, prebendaryes /, muncke pencyons /, morowe mas prestes /, vnlerned curattes /, prestes of gyldes and of fraternytees, or brotherhedes /, rydinge chaplaynes / and suche other ydle parsons /; whyche yf they be well noted /, and also what frute spryngethe of them, indyfferently valewed /, consydered /, and pondered, / it will appere manyfestly to all reasonable and godly wyttes /, that they do brynge noo maner commodyte, profett, or vtylyte, other spyrituall or temporall, to this your publycke wealthe. No /, no /! They be not onely no commodyte nor profett to the common wealthe /, but rather moche hynderance. And truly no lytle wasters /, spoylers /, and robbers /; and that of the most poore /, indygent, and neadye of youre louinge subiectes /, which be most craftely /, subtelly /, and vnrightuousely depryued of the charytable succoure and almes of many symple, vnlerned innocentes /, through a vayne hope and false confydence that theyr sowles shulde be releued and released of theyr paynes and tormentes dewe for theyr synnes /, when they be departed this worlde /, by the longe prayers of prestes. And (the more it is to be lamented) noo lytle nombre of your subiectes, through suche vngodly truste and confydence in masses and dyryges to be songe and celebrated for them when they be dead /, be greatly encoraged to lyue both wickedly towardes God /, and also vnfrutefully towardes the worlde /; lytle remembrynge and estemynge their vocacion & callinge, wherin God hath appoynted them to walke /, and moche lesse the extreame necessyte of

---

The country is overburdened with priests of one sort or another.

These idle parsons are no good,

but a harm to the State; they are robbers of the king's subjects, who are deprived of the alms of many in the hope that prayers avail for the dead.

Many are encouraged to live wickedly by an ungodly trust in masses and dirges.

AN IGNORANT PRIESTHOOD. 43

their Christen bretheren. This vayne hope in the longe prayers of prestes (no doubt, graciouse Lorde) is a greate occasyon of moche pouerte amongest the poore and neady of this yowr realme. For the spedy remedy of this pouerte amongest your louinge subiectes /, and the vtter suppressyon of suche vayne hope in the prayers of prestes to be made for your subiectes when they be deade /, whiche is the greate cause of this myserable pouerte /, it may please your Magestye, of your accustomed goodnes, to call to your graciouse remembrance that all the people, of this your regyon, be subiect vnto yowr gracyouse power /, rule /, and dominion, as vnto their supreme hedd and gouernowre, dewly by God appointed to gouerne them onely durynge their naturall lyues /; but when it pleaseth God to take their sowles owt of this myserable worlde, / than yowr Grace is dyscharged of all gouernance /, cure, & charge ouer them /, as of suche which, after their death, doo not appertayne to yowr Grace /, nor be of your kyngedome /; but onely of the kyngedome of God /, vnder his gouernance, prouisyon, and rule. Into the whiche kyngedome, nother your Grace nor noo other erthely prynce, maye lawfully vsurpe or take any rule, prouisyon, care or gouernance /, for the sowles entered therunto. Seinge that your Grace haue no auctoryte nor power ouer the sowles departed /, yow be not onely dyscharged to gouerne, to care, or to prouyde for them, beinge deade /; but moche rather to prouyde that they maye not be deceyued so vnder the coloure of longe prayre /, but that they may be taught syncerely Godds Worde, whyle they be lyuinge vnder your subiection, so that they maye beleue constantly and lyue godly /; and then, by Christes promesse, hell gates shall not prevayle ageinste them /: moche lesse they shall haue any neade of suche straunge succoure and helpe of men /, nothinge appointed nor tawght by Godds Worde,

The hope in the prayers of priests is a cause of poverty amongst the poor.

While the people live they are under the dominion of the king;

when they die, the king is discharged of his care over them.

No earthly prince may usurp authority over the dead.

The king must see that the people are not deceived; they must be taught,

and then the gates of hell shall not prevail against them.

5

to be profitable or necessary for their sowles after their death. Wherfore, I mistruste not but that your Magestye, when you shall next intreate for the reformacion of the enormytyes & abuses sprongen vp in the Christen religio*n* /, yow will godly reforme suche abuse and dissembled couetuousenes /, and certeynely beinge no godly remedy nor helpe for sowles departed, which hathe noo strengthe nor effycacy of Gods Worde /, which is the very trew fowndacio*n* of all the Christen religion and helpe for sowles. And, in *the* meane season, I doo no lesse thynke, and also pray hartely to God, that your Magestye will prouide and make ordinaunce /, that all suche landes and possessyons, wherevpon so many ydle hypochrytes and deceyuers be greate burdeyn & charge to your realme /, which hytherto haue lyued vngodly and vnprofytablely /, maye, from henceforthe, be partly conuerted to the supportation and mayntenaunce of common scoles /, wherby errours crepte vp through ingnora*n*ce maye be through knowlege repressed /, and godly lernynge and knowleage more ple*n*tuousely planted and admynistred /; and partely that your poore louing subiectes maye be more mercyfully releued & succoured /, whyle they lyue vnder your subiection, charge, and gouernaunce. This godly dystrybution (most prudent Soueraigne) of the landes and possessions, ordeyned and appoy*n*ted for the counforte, soccoure, and helpe of yowr poore louinge and lyuinge subiectes /, is moche more consonante and agreable to Godds Worde, and more certeyne dyscharge of your Graces co*n*scyence, then to suffer the same possessyons to be vngodly caste awaye and consumed vnder suche false colowre and pretence to releue sowles departed /; of whom your Magestye haue nother cure nor charge /, nor can not assure to them, by Godds Worde, through suche longe prayers of prestes, relesse of paynes after their deathe /, or any other ayde, coun-

When you treat for the reformation of abuses,

reform all which have no strength in God's Word.

All lands and possessions taken from religious houses should be given to support common schools,

and to relieve the poor while they live under the king's subjection.

This would be better than to allow these possessions to be used under a pretence of relieving departed souls.

forte, or succoure. For, with owt any doubt (gracyouse Lorde) yf suche hyred prayers had ben godly and necessary for the sowles departed /, other Christ or his Apostelles wolde haue taught it /, or, at the leaste, haue praysed or practysed it /; & not so manifestly reproued & thretened it /, sayeng :—" Beware of them whiche deuoure wyddowes howses, vnder coloure of longe prayers /; theyr iudgment shalbe moche longer." In all the Newe Testament there is no mencyon made of any suche offycer, nor offyce instytuted, nor appoynted, to praye for the deade. And yet all men, I thynke, will confesse that the truethe of Godes Worde was most syncerely set forthe and preached in the tyme of Chryste & of his Apostles /; in whose tyme there was no suche craftye lernynge publyshed nor tawght by them /, nor longe tyme after. But then men stablysshed and grownded their religion and hope of healthe vpon Godds Worde /, whiche teacheth vs *that* who so beleueth is saued, and hathe no neade of longe, prystishe prayers /; and who so beleueth not /, shallbe condempned. Betwene these extreame contraries there is no meane /; as Saint Augustijn saieth. Wherfore I exhorte all them (whiche contrary to all Holy Scriptures) truste to the thyrde place, and there to haue release of paynes through *the* longe prayers of prestes;/ that they wolde geue ouer suche fayned fantasye of me*n* (subtylly ymagined only through insaciable couetuousenes of ambiciouse prestes, to gett mony therwith to mainteyne their vngodly lustes /, and to lyue ydlely and delycately) and to truste rather to the sure and infallyble trewthe of Godds Worde /, which, wit*h*owt doubte, is to repent and beleue /, and vtterly to forsake all synne /; and than constantly to trust to Goddes promesse of mercy. Here manifestly apperethe, soueraygne Lorde /, in what miserable blyndnes the most parte of this your realme haue lo*n*ge tyme be[n]

If prayers for the dead had been necessary, Christ would have said so.

Marc. xij.

There is no mention of them in the New Testament.

The Apostles taught no such thing.

He who believes has no need of priests' prayers.

Note here S. August. in his boke entyteled Hypognosticon. fol. ix. Wherefore I exhort all who believe in Purgatory to leave their vain fancy,

and trust to the infallible truth of God's Word.

led /, yea, and allmost drowened, through the longe custome vsed theryn. Who is it that can not lament (I saye) this deplorate & miserable sorte of blynde shepherdes? Be not they bowght with the same pryce wherwith we be bought, to be membres of one bodye, wherof Christ is heade? If we be membres of one bodye, certenly we can not then but taste and feale, not onely their euill /, but also the lamentable estate of al other caste awaye through them. Lorde, I truste the punyshement is past wherwith thow haste threatened the worlde to be punished with hunger and thryste; not with hungre and thryste of breade and drincke /, but for lacke of hearinge thy Worde. Yt is nowe tyme, Lorde, to shewe thyne accustomed goodnes & mercye /, for the whiche we doo dayly and hartely praye /, sayenge: "Through the tender mercy of God, wherwith he hathe vysyted vs /, geue light to vs which sytt in darcknes and in the shadowe of deathe /, to guyde our feate into the waye of peace." Also it is a daungerouse thinge to admitte one to be a spirituall pastoure, whose professyon and study all his youthe hathe ben in decrees and popishe lawes. For suche a study, for the most parte, ingendereth a popishe harte. If any suche be admitted to be a pastoure /, he shal not onely, other secretly in confessyon or by some other crafty meanes /, poyson his flocke with mans tradycions & popishe doctrine /, but also shall augment the popishe power /; for the abrogacion *wherof yowr Grace and yowr honorable Councell haue taken greate paynes & travayle. Nowe, eftsones, I truste that all men, which reade this lytle boke, shall perceyue therby what inconuenyence & dampnable euyll enseweth the vngodly presentacyon and admyssyon of the vnlerned in Godds Worde /, and carnall prestes to spyrituall offices.[2]

[1] This page is transposed in the orig., and stands where the next one should be.   [2] Orig. officers.

And althoughe suche patrons haue lytle zeale and loue to the common and publike wealthe /, yet for the synguler and carnall loue which they beare to their clerkes (whom they addycte and bynde surely to eternall dampnacion /, if they geue them suche spyrituall offyces /, whiche they neyther can nor will execute and perfourme) or for the tender zeale and loue which they haue to the sowles so derely bought with Christes bloode /, they wyll, wyth all circumspection, proue theyr clerkes that they be not onely well lerned in Gods Worde /, but that they also haue taken greate paynes in preachynge the same /, and that they haue also lyued accordinge to their preachynge. Suche experyment and proue was commaunded to be made of weddowes /, before they were admytted to lyue vpon the charge of the congregacyon, as it appearethe in Tymothy. *Muche more than euydent and sure proue of pastours (whose offyce is soo necessarie) shulde be hade and made before they be admytted to their spyrituall offyce and charge. And, althoughe the election of the byshop and of other spirituall pastors in euery poynte be hade and done accordinge as I haue before wryten /, yet (most dread soueraigne Lorde) I see two fowle deformytes and grete lamentable myschefes annexed to the vocacyon & offyce of byshops /, which, not refourmed, will poyson and vtterly corrupte the godly vocacion and electyon of the sayd byshops. The one infection and pestylent poyson is there greate lordships and domynions, with the yerely prouentes of the same. Whiche hathe so fasshyoned them in proude countenaunces and worldely behauoure /, that nowe they be moste lyke to heathen prynces, and moste vnlyke vnto Christe /, althoug[h]e they wolde be esteemed of all men to be his trewe successours /; yet poore Christ

Although patrons have little zeal,

it is hoped they will examine clerks, and so ascertain whether they are well learned.

i. Ti. v.
[* leaf 21, back] [1]

If bishops be properly elected,

yet there are two more evils belonging to them :—

1. Their great lordships, and the rents arising from them.

They live like heathen princes,

---

[1] This page from here is transposed; in the original it precedes the one just given.

SECULAR DUTIES OF BISHOPS.

but "Poor Christ" had not where to lay His head. They have castles, parks full of deer; fish-ponds, and other pleasures.

sayethe :—" The foxes haue hooles /, the byrdes of the ayre haue neastes /, but *th*e sonne of man hathe not wherin to laye his head." But oure byshops haue gorgeouse & su*m*ptuouse buylded howses, maners, & castelles, pleasauntely set abowte w*ith* parckes, well replenished with deare /; warrens swarminge full of conyes /, and fyshe pooles well stored with dyuerse kyndes of fyshes. And not onely these commodities and pleasures /, but also diuerse other pleasures. Howe this lordely and worldely byshoplike estate agreeth with Christes wordes /; I thinke a man can not reasonably conyecture or ymagen, by theyr countenaunce and lyuinge /, that they be Christes trewe disciples. The

2. They have too many cures and too much worldly business. They manage their estates in all their details;

other myschefe and euill is, that they haue to many worldly cures and busenes. For to these maners and lordeshipes belonge many tenauntes /, for whose leases to be made, fynes and haryottes to be appointed and taken /, amercyamentes to be assessed, taxed, & also forgeuen and dispenced /, there be noo fewe sutes made

must hear testamentary causes, divorce suits,

to my lorde byshope /; also the hearinge of testamentorye causes /, dyuorses /, causes of matrimonye /, of sclaunders /, of leacherye, / adultery /, and pu*n*-

and such other matters not belonging to their vocation. My lord is so occupied with these things that he cannot find time to study or to preach.

yshement of bawedrye /; and suche other bu*mm*e courte matters, wherof not one belong to his offyce & vocation appointed by Godds Worde. My Lorde Byshope is so occupyed & vnquyeted /, that he hathe noo leasure to studye nor to preache Gods Worde. But suche affayres and worldly busynes, nothing perteyninge to his vocation, be very greate hynderance and lett to my Lorde Byshop, that he can not applye

Mat. v[i].

hym to exercyse his owne offyce. "For no man can serue two masters," sayeth Christ. The Apostles thought it not iuste and equall to prouide for the

Art. vi.

necessary lyuinge of the poore /, leauinge Godds Worde vntawght. But my Lorde Byshoppe, doinge these things, nothing perteyninge to his office /, thincketh

that he hathe exactely done his offyce. From these
greate maners commeth yerely, greate rentes, pleasures, *His great income*
& profettes /; which, althowghe they be the good crea- *might entice his heart to trust in*
tures of God /, yet thabundaunce of them (beinge *it and so corrupt him.*
where they be more impedyment than helpe) be a
greate occasyon of corrupcion in the vser of them.
And, peraduenture, they wolde allure and intyse a
byshops harte to truste in them and so corrupte hym /,
as the Scripture sayeth :—" Blessed is the ryche, *"Blessed is the*
which is founde withowt blemyshe, & hathe not gone *rich who is found without*
after golde, nor hoped in money and treasures /; where *blemish, and has not gone after*
is there suche a one and we shall commende hym and *gold:*
call hym blessed /; for greate things dothe he amonge *for he does*
his people." And if my Lorde Bysshoppe shulde geue *great things among his*
the superfluyte of his goodes to the poore (whose *people."*
goodes iustely they be) as the prophete Ezay sayethe /, *Esa. iij.*
than my Lorde shulde lacke them to furnyshe his
lordely countenaunce /; and so my Lorde shulde loose
his lordely honoure and prayse of the worlde. Wherfore, as these superfluouse possessions be annexed to
estates of bysshops, by mans vayne fantasye and not
by Gods Worde /, so my Lorde Byshoppe wyll other *The bishops use*
keape them to make hym more fryndes/, remembrynge *their riches to make friends,*
that "ryches makethe many fryndes /, but the poore
is forsaken of his neyghbowre"/; or deuyse the exspence
of them contrary to Godes Worde /, other to make *or to bribe those*
sure fryndes in the courte aboute the kynge, to obteyne *about the court;*
more promocions & benefices /, or in curiouse buyld- *or else in building,*
inge /, sumptuouse and delycate fare /, well appareled *fine living,*
seruauntes /, tryme decked horses, to ryde pompecusely *servants, horses,*
lyke a lorde. Althoughe there were no auctorite to *and riding like lords.*
proue this /, yet the lordely countenaunce & fasshyon
of byshops /, yea, their common exercyse and also
practyse, can well proue and testyfye this playnely before the face of all men, which knoweth the lordely-
nes of bysshopps. As the prophete Ezay sayethe :— *Esa. iij.*

THE PRIDE OF THE BISHOPS.

All which are opposed to the saying of the Apostle, i. Ti. vi. "When we have food and raiment let us be content."

Lu. xxij.

Peter tells bishops to feed the flock of God;

taking the oversight willingly and with a godly mind.

But the proud countenance of our bishops is contrary to all this.

Math. xij.

And so long as this is so,

they cannot sincerely and truly Rom. x. preach.

Ioan. xx.[1]

Christ was sent to preach, and He sent His disciples to do the same.

"The chaungynge of their countenaunce bewrayeth them /, yea they declare theyr owne synnes them selfes as Sodomytes /, and hyed them not." Doo not these thinges fayntely agree with the sayenge of theyr predecessour, Paule the Apostle, which sayeth:—" When we haue foode and raymente we muste be contented?" Is not this lordely honoure dyrectely agaynste Chrystes wordes /, which sayethe :—" The kynges of nacyons raygne ouer them / and they that haue auctoryte ouer them are called graciouse lordes. But yow shall not be so." Also Peter speakethe to his trewe successoures sayenge :—" Feade yow Christes flocke as muche as lyeth in yow /, takynge the ouersyght of them; not as compelled therunto /, but wyllyngelye /, after a godly sorte /; nor for the desyer of fylthy luker /, but of a good mynde /; not as thoughe yowe were lordes ouer the paryshes /, but that yowe be an example to the flocke /, and that withe good will." But owre lordely byshops estate, and proude countenaunce of lyuynge (as it is nowe vsed) is contrarye to Godes Worde /, as it appearethe by these wordes:—" But yow shall not be so." And also by these sayengs :— " Not as thoughe yow were lordes ouer the paryshes." And Chryst sayethe :—" He that is not with me /, is agaynste me." Wherefore, so longe as they raigne so lordely in the clergie, contrary to Godds Worde /, so longe be they againste God. And so longe as they be agaynste God /, they be not sente from God /, and then can they not preache trewly and syncerely his worde. " For howe can they preache excepte they be sente?" sayeth Paul. Christe was sente to preache, as it appearethe. Marc. i., Luce. iiij., and Ezaye. lxi. And Christe sayeth to all his trewe dysciples :—" As my Father sente me /, so I do sende yow." And commaundeth also all his Apostles, & trewe successors of the Apostles, to

[1] Orig. .ij.

NEGLECT OF SPIRITUAL DUTIES.

preache the Gospell to the holle worlde, and not lordely to raigne in the clergye. Whom Paul teacheth to be as mynisters /, sayeng : "Lett a man this wise esteame vs /, euyn as the mynisters of Christe and the stuardes of the secretes of God." To preache the Gospell therfore (most gracyouse and prudente Lorde) is the trewe vocacyon and offyce of all godly byshops /, parsons /, vycars, and of other shepherdes /; and not to be enbasadowrs to prynces, / nor to be iudges to here matters of contencyon, / testamentarye causes /, dyuorses /, sclaunders, / bawdery /, and suche other. Your Grace hathe, of your laye fee, suffycient bothe in lerninge, and wysedome, and of good conscyence, to here and iudge suche causes and varyaunces /; remyttynge byshops to attende their offyce and vocacyon by God (and not by man) appoynted. And therfore they shulde not excercyse any other offyce than God hathe appoynted to them. For "no man can serue two masters." And if byshops and other pastoures wolde dyligently execute theyr vocacyon and offyce /, moche fewer of these matters of contencyon shalbe in vre and experience, other to be harde or iudged. Seinge the Scriptures commaundeth so ernestly euery man to walke as he is called, many Christen men meruell gretly why the byshops desyre and procure so greadely to exercyse the offyce perteyninge to an other vocacyon /, and to leue their vocacyon and offyce (appoynted by God to them to be exercysed) not executed nor performed and done. Verely bycause they loue the glorye of men / more then the glorye of God. And surely euen as Cayphas and Annas, beinge byshops, and exercysynge the offyce of seculer and temporall iudges, ded iudge Christ to be crucifyed /, so owr byshops, so longe as they, contrarye to their callynge, doo exercyse the offyce of temporall iudges /, so longe shall they persecute Christe and his

i. Cor. iiij.

To preach the gospel is the vocation of all bishops and parsons,

and not to be ambassadors or judges.

There are plenty of lawyers, learned and wise enough to hear and judge such causes, leaving bishops to attend to their own duties.

Mat. vi.

Men marvel why bishops strive after other offices, and leave their own vocation unperformed.

Ioan. xii.[1]
Verily it is because they love the praise of men more than the praise of God.

---
[1] Orig. ix.

FASHIONS IN DRESS.

There is business enough to employ them in their own office.

membres /, and studye to suppresse his worde /, and not to preache the same. Haue not they busynes suffycyent, wherwith to occupye them in their owne offyce? If they wolde loke well therunto /, doo not they see on euery syde detestable synne raigne throughowt all this your realme? Is there not suche excesse and costelynes of apparell /, bycause of dyuersyte and chaunge of fasshyons, that scarce a worshipfull mans landes, which in tymes paste was wonte to fynde and maynteyne twenty or thirty tall yowemen /, a good plentyfull howsholde for the releyfe and counforte of many poore and neadye /; and the same nowe is not suffycyent and able to maynteyne the heyre of the same landes /, his wiffe /, her gentle woman or mayde /, two yowmen /, and one lackey? The pryncypall cause herof is their costly apparell /, and specially their manyfolde and dyuerse chaunges of fasshyons whiche the man, and specially the woman, muste weare vpon bothe headde and bodye. Somtyme cappe /, somtyme hoode /; nowe the Frenshe fasshyon /, nowe the Spanyshe fasshyon /; than the Italyan fasshyon /, and then the Myllen fasshyon /; so that there is noo ende of consumynge of substaunce, and that vaynely, and all to please the prowde folyshe man and womens fantasye. Hereof spryngethe great myserye and neade. The fathers consumynge theyr goodes in vayne / pryde /, and wanton lustes (called vpon by yowr Grace to serue yowr Magestye for the defence of this yowr realme) haue not to doo their dewtye /; wherby they be compelled to sell theyr landes /, or els to burdeyne their fryndes /, or els to daunger them selfe in dette to many. Hereof rysethe it that the father is compelled to declare his will vpon hys landes to be executed after his deathe (when he can not occupye the same hym selfe) for the aduauncement and helpe of his children, and the payment of his dettes /, whom easely he myght in his lyffe

Sin reigns everywhere

Costly apparel and change of fashions have made men who once could maintain 20 or 30 yeomen,

and comfort many poor, now scarce able to maintain their own households.

These two things, costly apparel and varying fashions, especially of the women, are the chief cause of this altered state of things.

Men are compelled to sell their lands,

or get in debt.

They have to burden their lands with provision for children who should have been provided for during life.

haue aduaunced, holpen, and dyscharged /, yf suche ryotuouse expenses had ben auoyded. The prophete Osee sayethe:—"There is noo trewethe /, no mercye /, *Ose. iiij.* no knowleage of God in earthe /; cursynge /, lyenge / murdre, thefte /, adulterye, hathe broken in" /; and yet doo owre shepherdes holde theyr peace. What com- *Drunkenness,* messacyon /, dronckenes /, detestable swearinge by all *swearing by Christ's Body,* the partes of Christes bodye (and yet callynge them in *"hunting oaths,"* scorne "huntinge othes") extorcyon /, pryde /, couet- *pride, and vice* uousenes /, and suche other detestable vyce, raigne in *reign in the realm,* this yowr realme /; agaynste the whiche owre byshops, *against which* and other pastoures, shulde contynually crye owt /, as *bishops and pastors should* the Prophete sayethe:—"Crye nowe as lowed as thow *cry aloud and Esa. lviii.[1]* canste /, leaue not of /, lyfte vp thy voyce lyke a trom- *spare not.* pett /, and shewe my people their offences, and the howse of Iacob their synnes." But, alas! they be- *But, alas! they* come bothe blynde and dome /, as the Prophete say- *are blind and dumb,* ethe:—"His watchmen are all blynde; they haue all *Esaye lvi.[2]* together noo vnderstandinge /, they are all dome dogges, not able to barcke /; they are slepye /, folyshe are they, and lye snortinge /. They are shameles dogges *and shameless.* that be neuer satysfyed. The shepherdes also in lyke maner haue no vnderstandinge /; but euery man turn- ethe his owne waye /, euery one after his owne couet- uousenes, with all his powre." What is the cause that *Why don't the* they doo not execute this their offyce? Other bycause *bishops execute their office?* they can not /, or bycause they haue somoche worldely busynes that they will not, apply them selfes to per- fourme bothe. Or els they be afrayed to speake the trwethe /, lest they shulde dysplease men. Whom Paul reproueth sayenge: "If I shulde please men, I *Gal. i.* shulde not be the seruaunte of Christe." Also the Prophete sayethe:—"God breakethe the bones of them *Psal. lij.[3]* whiche studye to please men /; they be confounded /,

[1] Orig. v.   [2] Orig. lxvi.
[3] 53rd in A. Version.

MISCHIEFS ARISING FROM THE

They love their possessions;

they will not displease men;

they will maintain their pride, and will continue in it;

Esa. [lx]vj.

and so long as they continue in wealth and honour they will not do their duty, but rather persecute the Bible which declares what their duty is.

When the Pope was first endowed with great possessions, a voice was heard— "Now poison is cast into the Church of God."

So long as honour and wealth are annexed to bishoprics,

because the Lorde dispyseth them." Notwithstandynge, owr byshops loue so well their greate domynions, wherby they maynteyne their lordely honoure /, that they will not dysplease men with preachynge the treuth /, lest they shulde then loose their greate possessyons /; and, consequently, their lordely glorye. But surely as longe as they possesse theyr greate domynions /, so longe they wyll contynewe and maynteyne their pryde. And so longe as they contynewe in pryde /, so longe they shall not receyue the Holy Ghoste /, whiche shall teach them to speake the treuthe. "For vpon whom shall my Sprete reaste" (sayeth the Prophete Esaye) "but vpon the meake and lowely /, and vpon hym which fearethe my sayengs." Also the Prophete sayeth: "God resysteth the prowde /, and vnto the meake and lowely he geuethe his grace." Wherfore, so longe as the byshops contynewe in this worldely wealthe and honowre /, so longe will they neuer do their dewtye and offyce /; but rather persecute the Worde of God whiche declarethe and shewethe what is their offyce and their dewtye. And so longe as they do not exercyse their offyce and vocatyon /, but doo persecute the Worde and suche as syncerely preache the same /, so longe shall synne increase. "For if the eye be wicked /, all the body shalbe full of darcknes." For euen as at suche tyme when the Byshoppe of Rome was fyrste endowed with greate possessyons /, a voyce was harde /, seyinge :—" Nowe venome and poyson is caste and shed forthe into the churche of God." In lykewyse, no doubt, most godly Gouernoure /, semblable voyce and sayenge maye be veryfyed in and vpon all the churche of Englande /, sythen yowr byshops were endowed with so greate possessyons and lordely dominions. No doubt, gracyous Lorde /, so longe as grete lordely domynions /, worldely honours and wealthe /, be anexed and knyt to the vocacyon and

offyces of byshops and other pastours /, these myscheues *these mischiefs will follow.*
& inconuenyences shall euer ensue & folowe. Fyrste
the moste prowde and ambycyouse /, the moste couet- *The proudest will seek the*
uouse and wycked, / which other by money, frendshyp, *benefice for its*
or flattery, can obtayne the benefyce /, wyll laboure *honours,*
with all study and polycye to gett the benefice, / only
for the worldely honoure, and not for the zeale and
loue which he shulde haue to enstructe and teache the *and not to teach*
people commytted to his cure and charge. And for *the people;*
the profett which belongethe and apperteynethe to the
same benefyce /, they wyll dyssemble humylyte and *he will feign humility, and*
despeccyon of all worldely profettes and pleasures /, so *seem to despise all worldly profits*
colorablye and subtelly /, that yt shall be very harde *and pleasures.*
for youre Magestye, or any other hauynge aucthoryte,
to geue benefyces, to perceyue them. And when they *But when he has obtained it every*
haue obteyned the benefyce /, than euery Christen man *Christian will*
shall well perceyue that he hathe not entered in by the *perceive he has not entered in*
dore; that is, for the zeale and loue, to doo and execute *by the door,*
the offyce /, but hathe clymmed vp and assended by a
nother waye; / that ys, for the luker and honoure
annexed to the offyce. And than certenly, whosoeuer
assendeth and enterethe in by a nother waye /, can not *and is therefore only a thief and*
be but a thefe /, by daye and by nyght; / whose study *a robber,*
and laboure muste be to steale /, kyll /, and to destroy. *whose study must be to steal,*
As Christe (whose wordes muste euer be true) sayethe: *kill, and destroy.*
—" The thefe commethe not but to steale, / to kyll /, *Ioan. x.*
and to destroye." So that, so longe as so moche
worldely profett and honoure belongethe to the benefyce, so longe wyll he that, for wante and lacke of
lernynge can not doo the offyce /, and also the moste
couetuouse and proude, / wyll laboure to haue the
offyce /, whereby the people commytted to his cure /, *The people will be untaught,*
shall not onely be vntawght[1] /, and not lerned in Gods *and those who would teach*
Worde /, but also all they which can preache and
teache Godds Worde and loue the same, / by suche

[1] Orig. vntawgth.

a worldely wolfe /, shall be extremely persecuted and tormented. For he can not but steale /, kyll /, and destroye /, and vtterly abhore /, and hate the godly /, as Christe sayethe :—" Yf you were of the worlde /, the worlde wolde loue his owne. But because you be not of the worlde /, but I haue chosen you from the worlde /, therfore the worlde dothe hate you." No doubt a man shall moche rather vpon thornes gather grapes /, and vpon brambles and bryres gather fygges, / than of soche gredy theues to haue any Chrysten relygyon, other setforthe /, preached, / or stablyshed. Wherfore (moste redoubted Prynce) seinge that theyr greate possessyons /, ryches /, worldely offyces /, cures /, and busynes /, be the impedyment and let that they do not execute theyr vocacyon and offyce /, whiche is so godly, profytable, and necessarye for this yowr common wealthe /; yowe beinge owr soueraigne Lorde and Kynge (whom God hathe called to gouerne this yowr realme /, and to redresse the enormytyes and abuses of the same), by all iustyce and equyte are bounden to take awaye from byshoppes and other spirytuall shepherdes suche superfluyte of possessyons, and ryches, and other seculer cures, busynes, and worldely offyces /, whiche be the cause of moche synne in them /: and no lesse occasyon whereby they be letted to execute their offyce /, to the greate losse and hynderance of moche faythe, vertue, and goodnes /, which myght be admynistred to your subiectes /, through the trew preachynge of Godes Worde. And that done /, than circumspectly to take heade that none be admytted to be pastoures, / but suche as can preache, and haue preached syncerely Godes Worde. And all suche as will not /, to remoue them from theyr cures. This godly ordre obserued in the electyon of spirituall pastoures /, and the pestylent poyson moued and taken away from theyr vocatyon /, faithe shall increase /, and synne shall decrease /; trewe

obedience shall be obserued wyth all humylite, to your
Magestye and to the hygher powers
by your Grace appoynted in office.
Cyuile quyetnes, reste, and pea- — *peace shall be established, and God shall be honoured.*
ce shalbe stablyshed /, God shal
be feared, honoured, and loued /, whiche is theffec-
te of all Chri-
sten lyuin-
ge.
(👉)

O Lorde, saue our moste soueraygne Lorde, Kynge — *O Lord, save the king; may he once feel what we suffer from these tyrants.*
Henry the Eyght /; and graunte that he may ones
throughly feale and perceyue what myserable calamyte,
sorowe, & wretchednes we suffer now in these dayes a
brode in the countre /, by these vnlerned /, popyshe /,
and moste cruell tyrauntes /, euen the very enemyes of
Chrystes crosse /; whose payne shall be withowt ende /,
whan we shall lyue in ioye for euer. Graunte yet
ones agayne, I say, goode Lorde, and moste mercyfull
Father, through thy Sone Ihesus Christe /, that whan
his Grace shall knowe and perceyue (by thy gyfte & — *Grant that when he knows their ways he may redress them.*
goodnes) theyr most detestable wayes in mysusynge thy
heretage /, that he wyll ernestly go a boute to se a
redresse a monge them /; and to the penytent and con-
tryte in harte to shewe his accustomed goodnes /, and
to the other his iustyce /, accordinge to Saynt Paules
doctryne /, and his Graces lawes.

And, moste dreade Soueraygne (with all humylyte and
humblenes of harte), I beseche your Grace / (accordinge — *I beseech your Grace to accept my supplication*
to your accustomed goodnes), to take this my rude

supplycacyon to the beste /, as a frute of my obedyence /, wheryn I haue not dyssembled /, but haue opened fully vnto your Grace the grounde and very bottome of my hart; / not of any grudge, euyll wyll, or malyce that I beare to any spirytuall shepherde (God I take to recorde), but onely for the glory of God /, the honoure of your Grace /, and the wealthe and profett of your moste naturall and louinge subiectes.

as a fruit of my obedience,

and not of malice to any spiritual shepherd.

FINIS.

¶ Enprynted in the yeare of our Lorde .M. CCCCC. xliiij. in the moneth of Decembre.

(☞)

A Supplication of the Poore Commons.

¶ *Prouerbes .xxi. Chapiter.*

¶ Who so stoppeth his eare at the criynge of the poore, he shall crye hym selfe, and shall not be heard.

¶ To the most victorious
Prynce Henry the viii. by the Grace of God
Kyng of Englande, Fraunce, & Ireland;
Defender of the Fayth, and Supreme
Head of the Churche of England,
and Ireland, immediatly next
vnto God: hys humble and
most faythfull Subiectes
of the Realme of En-
gland, wysh lyfe
euerlastyng.

Pituously complaineth the pore commons of this your Maiesties realme, greatly lamentyng their owne miserable pouertie; and yet muche more the most lamentable and more then wretched estate of their chyldren and posterite. Whose myserie, forsene and throughly considered, is and ought of very nature, to be more dolorous and sorowful vnto euerye naturall hert then that which we our selues feale and sustayne. Not many yeres tofore, your Highnes poore subiectes, the lame, and impotente creatures of this realme, presented your Highnes with a piteful and lamentable complaint, imputyng the head and chiefe cause of their penury and lacke of reliefe, vnto the great & infinite nombre of valiant and sturdy beggers which had, by their subtyll and crafty demaner in begging, gotten into their handes more then the third

The commons complain of their miserable condition, especially of their extreme poverty.

Some years ago the poor, lame, and impotent presented a petition against valiant and sturdy beggars,

who had got into their hands more than a third of

part of the yearely reuenewse and possessions of this your Highnes realme. Wher vpon (as it semed) your Hyghnes (sekynge a redresse and reformation of thys greate and intollerable enormitie,—as a merciful father ouer this your natural country; moued wyth pitie towardes the miserable and pittiful nombre of blind, lame, lazar, & other the impotent creatures of this your realme) hath, wyth most ernest diligence, supplanted, and, as it were, weeded out, a greate numbre of valiaunt and sturdye monckes, fryers, chanons, heremites, and nunnes. Which disguised ypocrites, vnder the name of the contempt of this world, wallowed in the sea in the worldes wealth. And to the entent your louing & obedient subiectes might the better be able to releue the neadie & impotent creatures, you toke from them the greate numbre of gilted beggers, whose holines was so fast roted in the hertes of vs your pore commons, through the false dilusions of the forsayd sturdy & valiant beggers, that we wold not stick to go an .C. myles on our bare fete to seke one of them, that we might not only bestow our almes vpon them, but also do them reuerence and honour none other wise then if they had bene very gods. Yea, when your Hyghnes had ordeyned that al these forsayd beggers shulde be vtterly abolished, neuer to deceyue vs of our almes anye more, we, like men alwaies brought vp in folish supersticion of these false Phariseis & flateryng hypocrites, knewe not the obedience that we owe to you, our natural and most rightful Prince, but in-continent fel in an vprore criyng, " Our holi dayes, abbayes & pylgrimages!" None o[t]her wise than the Ephesians dyd agaynst the elect vessell of God, Sancte Paule, whan he sayd, "They are not godes, which be made with handes," and as the Iewse did against holy Steuen, whan he sayd that "God dwelleth not in an house made with mans hand." Yea, had not God wrought

on your parte, in apeasing that sturdy thronge, this
realme had, euen then, ben like to haue bene vtterly
decayed. For euen those whome your Highnes had
called to-gither to assiste you in that daungerous tyme,
were (for the moste parte) so bente to the opinion of
the other, that many of them woulde not stike to say,
"When we shal come to the battaile,—we know what
we haue to do." But nowe (the Lorde be thanked therfore) that your Highnes hath finished that your godly
purpose, without bloudshede of your poore commones,
and that the Worde of God hath ben so set furth &
taught by your command[m]ent, that euery man that
lusteth may therin learne his duitie and office ; we are
fully perswaded, that all such as resiste the pours,
whome God hathe ordeyned and appoynted to rule &
gouerne the multitude of thys worlde, do not resyste
man, but God. Be you certayne therfore (most
graciouse Prince) that we (your most obedient subiectes) walkyng in the fear of the Lord, wyl not from
hense forth (so long as the knowledge of Godes Worde
shall reigne amongeste vs) attempt any such so diuilishe
enterprise, as to rebel agaynst your Highnesse, our most
natural Souerayne and Leage Lorde ; either for our for-
fathers popyshe tradicions, or other oure owne fantasti-
cal dreams; not withstandynge that the remenaunt of
the sturdy beggers (not yet weaded out) do daylye, in
theyr writynges, counsels, and preachynges, stere vs
thereunto. For what meane they in their sermons
when they lament the greate discord and myserable
estate of this our tyme, wishynge that all thynge were
nowe as it was .xx. yeares since, but that they woulde
haue a Pope, pardons, lightyng of candels to images,
knockyng and knelyng to them, with runnyng hither
and thither on pilgremage ; besides the infinit number
of purgatory horseleches, on whom the vengeaunce of
God is so manifestly declared for their beastly buggery,

But you finished your purpose without bloodshed of the commons,

and now we are convinced that to resist the powers is to resist God;

and, so long as we are taught by God's word, will never rebel again,

though we be tempted thereto by the beggars not yet weeded out.

that the very places where thei dwelt, ar not thought worthy to be the dwellinges of men, but the caues of bruit bestes and venemous wormes? Thei tell vs what vice, vncharitablenes, lacke of mercy, diuercitie of opinions, and other lyke enormites, haue raigned euer sence men had the Scripture in Englyshe. And what is thys other then to cause mens consciens to abhorre the same, as the onely cause and originall of all thys? Thei say that it sufficeth a laye man to beleue as thei teach, and not to meddle with the enterpretation of the Scriptures. And what meaneth that, but that thei would haue vs so blynd agayn, as we were when we would haue fought agaynst oure naturall Prynce, for the mayntenaunce of their popyshe traditions and purgatory patrimony? Thei cannot abyde this name, "the Word of God;" but thei wold haue the Scripture called the commaundement of God. And what meaneth this, but that thei are the same enemyes of God, whom that two edged sword shall destroy? Finally, thei haue procured a lawe, that none shal so hardy haue the Scripture in his house, onlesse he maye spend x. pound by yere. And what meaneth this, but that they would famysh the soules of the residue, witholdyng theyr food from them? We appeale to your Highnes iudgement in this behalfe, whither this lawe be indifferent or not. If none should be alowed meat in your Highnes house, but suche as were clothed in veluet, with chaines of gold about theyr neckes, what seruauntes wold your Maiestie haue shortly? What steruelynges would your seruauntes be aboue all other! For no man within your realme may refuse to do your Grace seruyce. Hath God put immortall soules in none other but in such as be possessioners of this world? Did not Chryst send word to Ihon the Baptist that the pore receyued the Gospell? And the Gospel that thei shutte vp from vs, was it not the writynges of poore fysher men and symple creatures, euen taken for the dregges of the worlde? Were not the setters furthe of it and the prophetes also, persecuted, tormented, and slayne? And why do these men disable them for readers of the Scriptures, that are not indued with the possessions of this worlde? Vndoutely (most gratious Souerayn) because they are the very same that shut vp the kyngdome of God before men; thei enter not them selues, nother suffre thei them to entre that wolde. They are lyke to a curre dogge liyng in a cocke of haye. For he wyll eate none of the heye hym selfe, nother suffer any other beast that commeth to eate therof. But some wyl peraduenture say, they were not all sturdy beggers that were in the Parlament when this lawe was stablished. For many of them, and the most parte were seculer men, and not of suche habilite that this lawe would permyt them to haue the Scripture in their houses. Wherfore, this lawe is in-different, and taketh not the Worde of God from vs; but we wyth oure ful consent haue committed it to them, in the sayde lawe limytted. Where vnto we aunswer, that, if we haue geuen it ouer from vs to the possessioners of this worlde, we may well be lykened to the Gedarites, Marke v., which desired Christ to departe from theyr country, and the lurking night birdes, which can not abyde the bryghte beames of the son. We may boldly affirme that what man soeuer doth wyttyngly and willingly forsake the knowledge of the lyuely Worde of God (the foode of our solles, and lyghte of oure footesteppes,) is none of the flock of Christ, forasmuch as his shepe heare his voyce, & reioyce in the same. Did thei that toke their names of anye philosopher, shut vp theyr masters doctrine from them selfe? Did thei not thynke them selues vnworthy to be named after their masters, vnlesse thei knewe their preceptes and rules? Did not the monkes, friers, and other the supersticious religious, employe all theyr

up, was written by poor fishermen. Those who preached it were persecuted and slain.

These men are like the dog in the manger.

But many who made this law were secular men, and not rich enough to benefit by it.

The law is indifferent.

We answer, If we gave it away from ourselves to the possessors of this world, we are like the Gadarenes.

We boldly affirm that whosoever forsakes God's word is none of His.

Those who took the name of any Philosopher, studied his teaching, and thought themselves unworthy of him unless they knew his precepts; and the monks

THE BIBLE OUGHT TO BE READ.

following this example, study to obtain a knowledge of their statutes.

studye to knowe their rules and statutes? Do not the Coelginers at this daye set the boke of theyr statutes at libertie, streightlye commaundyng eche felowe vnder payne of punishemente to employ them, to haue the through knowledge of the same? And shold we glory to be the flocke of Chryst, and to be called of him

And shall we exclude ourselves from a knowledge of Christ's laws which we must follow, on pain of damnation?

Christians, when we do willyngly and wittyngly exclude our selfe from the knowlege of the rule which he hathe commaunded vs to folowe, on payne of dampnation of oure soules? Would your Hyghnes thynke that man were willyng to do your commaundement, that would not diligently reade ouer your Highnes letters sent from you to certifie hym of youre wyll and pleasure in hys office? And what other thynge is the whole Scripture then the declar[at]ion of the wyl of God? Wer it lykely therfore, that we, excludyng our selues from the knowledge therof, shold be willyng to

If we have rejected God's offer, when He used your Highness to publish His word, in which we may learn His love towards us;

do his wyl? If we haue therfore reiected this merciful profer of our moost mercifull Father, when he vsed youre Hyghnes, as hys instrumente, to publyshe and set forthe hys moost lyuelycke Worde, wherin is declared the inestimable loue that he beare towardes vs, in that he gaue hys onelye Sonne to be an acceptable sacrifice for oure synnes; and the vnspekable mercy which caused him to accept vs as iust, euen for his Sonnes sake, without our workes or deseruinges; let vs

let us repent most humbly,

now humbly fal downe prostrate before his Maiestye, wyth perfecte repentance of this, the contempte of his mercifull gyfte; moost humbly besekinge hym, of his infinyte goodnes, tenderly to beholde the doloures of our hertes, for that we neglected so mercifull a profere;

and beseech Him to forget our obstinacy.

and to forget oure obstinacie ther in, geuynge your Hyghnes suche desire of oure saluation, that you wyll as fauorably restore vnto vs the Scripture in oure English tonge, as you dyd at the fyrst translation therof set it abrode. Let not the aduersaries take occasion

Don't let our enemies say the

THE BIBLE PLACED IN CHURCHES.

to say, the Bible was of a traytours settinge forthe, and not of your Hyghnes owne doynge. For so they reporte, that Thomas Cromwell, late Earle of Essex, was the chyfe doer, and not youre Hyghnes, but as led by him. All thys thei do to withdraw the mindes of vs (your Hyghnesses subiectes) from the readyng and study therof. Which thyng doth easely appere by the diligence they shewe in settyng furth and execution of your Hyghnes proclamations and iniunctions consernyng the same. For when youre Highnes gaue commaundement that thei shoulde se that there were in euery parysh churche, within thys your Highnes realme, one Byble at the least set at libertie, so that euery man myght frely come to it, and read therin, suche thynges as should be for his consolation, manye of this wicked generation, as well preystes as other their faythful adherentes, wuld pluck it other into the quyre, other elles into som pue, where pore men durst not presume to come. Yea, ther is no smale numbre of churches that hath no Byble at all. And yet not suffised with the withholdyng of it from the pore of their owne parishes, they neuer rested tyl they had a commaundement from your Highnes, that no man, of what degree so euer he wer, should read the Bible in the tyme of Goddes seruice (as they call it); as though the hearyng of theyr Latin lyes, and coniuryng of water and salte, were rather the seruice of God, then the study of his most Holy Worde, the onelye foode of our soules, and lyght of our fote steppes; wythout whiche no man can walke vpryghtly in perfect lyfe, worthy our name and profession.

This was theyr diligence in settynge forthe the Byble at your Hyghnesse commaundement. But when your Highnesse had diuised a proclamation for the burnynge of certen translations of the Newe Testament, they were so bold to burne the whole Bibles, because

Bible was set forth by the traitor Thomas Cromwell, and not by your Highness, except as led by him.

Your proclamation commanded that a Bible should be placed in every church throughout the realm, so that every man might read it, but many wished to put it into the choir, or into a pew where the poor man dare not come;

and they never rested till it was decreed that no man should read it during God's service, as they call it.

When your Highness gave orders for burning certain translations of the New Testament,

68 A NEW TRANSLATION PROMISED.

they burnt the whole Bible because the same men translated it.

they were of those mens' translations. And yf your Hyghnesse woulde enquire of them whoe toke the paynes in translatinge the Great Byble that your Highnes hath authorised, we thynke they coulde not, for verye shame, denie, but, euen agaynste theyr wylles, graunt, that those poore men, whose paines & greate trauayle they haue rewarded with fire and banishment, were the doers ther of. See, gratiouse Prince, how they play bopipe with your Highnes commaundementes, suppressinge, in al that they dare, the thyng that youre Highnesse hath authorised; euen as it were men that loked for a faire daye, which we trust, in the Lorde Iesu, they shall neuer see. As we herd say, they profered your Highnesse, that if it wolde please you to call in the Bible agayne (for as much as it was not faithfully tra*n*slated in al partes) they wold ouer see it, and with in .vii. yeres set it forth agayne. A wiles; we think they haue red the story of a certen man, who, beynge condemned to die, profered that, if he might haue his life, he would doo his prince such a pleasure as neuer man dyd, for hee woulde, wythin the space of .xiiii. yeres, teach him an ase to daunce. Where vpon he had his lyfe graunted him, vpon condition that yf he dyd not performe his promessed enterprise, that then he shoulde neuer the lesse suffer deathe. Thys done, he was demau*n*ded of one of his familiers, why he was so madde to take vppon him such an enterprise, so farre beyonde all reason and possibilytie? He answered, "my frend, hold the co*n*tent; I haue wrought wysly, for wyth in these xiiii. yeares, other the kynge, I, or the asse, shalbe dead; so that by thys meanes I shall escape thys reprochfull and shamfull death." So your byshopes (most victoriouse Prince) if they might haue gotten in the Bible for vii. yeres, they wolde haue trusted that by that tyme, ether, youre Highnes shoulde haue ben dead, or the Bible forgotten, or els

See how they play bo-peep with your Highness's commands, suppressing, where they dare, what you have allowed.

They wished the Bible called in, and promised a new translation in seven years.

In this they were like the criminal who saved his life

by promising to teach an ass to dance in 14 years.

They trusted that in that time your Highness would be dead, or the Bible forgotten,

THE OLD SERVICES ARE USED. 69

they them selues out of your Highnes reache, so that you should not haue had like power ouer them as you haue nowe. Wel, go to, we trust ere the vii. yeres be past, God shall reuaile vnto your Highnes moch more of theyr subtyll imaginations then we are worthy to know of. Moreouer, wil your Highnes se howe faythfully they dyd youre commaundement, when you appoynted two of them to ouer loke the translation of the Bible? They sayd they had done youre Highnes commaundement therin, yea, they set their names there vnto; but when they sawe the worlde som what lyke to wrynge on the other syde, they denyed it, and said they neuer medeled therewith, causyng the prynter to take out theyr names, which were erst set before the Bible, to certifie all men that thei had diligently perused it according as your Highnes had commaunded. One other poynt of theyr diligence your Highnes may note in the settyng furth and vsyng of youre Hyghnes Primer both in Englysh and Latin. And in the diligent readyng vnto the people, the exhortation to prayer, which you ordeyned and commaunded to be redde alwaies before the Prossession in Englysh. We thynk no man can blameles say, that euer he heard one of them reade it twyse ouer. Yea, when your Highnes was returned from youre victory done at Bullyn, they dyd what they coulde to haue called it in agayne. In so much that they caused all such parishes as they myght commaunde, to vse theyr olde Kyre Eleyson agayne. And yet to this daye, thei vse, on solempne feastes, to folow theyr olde ordinary, not withstandyng your Highnes commaundement. But when thei katch any thyng that soundeth to the contrary, it shall not escape so, we warrant you. It shalbe swynged in euery pulpyt wyth, "this is the Kynges gratious wyll; and yet these heretickes wylbe styll doyng in the Scriptures. A shomaker, a cobbler, a tayler, a boy not

or themselues out of your reach.

Two were appointed to overlook the translation,

and set their names to it, to testify they had done so;

afterwards they had their names omitted, saying they had never meddled with it.

They never read the exhortation to prayer, as commanded by your Highness,

and on Feast days use the old ordinary.

When they catch anything they like, it is "swinged" in every pulpit, as the king's gracious will.

PROVISION TO BE MADE FOR THE POOR.

They say how well disposed the people used to be;

how many hospitals were built, and colleges founded;

and would add, abbeys and chantries were then founded, if they dare.

If they had their way, building would be the best trade going.

We pray that their subtleties may always come to light before they prevail;

that these sturdy beggars be rooted out;

and that the tenth of every man's increase may go to the poor, as it was long before Christ, and long before the Law.

yet xx. yeres of age, shal not stycke to reproue that a lerned manne of xl. yeares studye shall affyrme in the declaration of Gods Word. O how godly wer the people disposed, when thei knew nothyng of the Scripture, but as thei were taught by profound clerkes and well lerned men! Then were there hospitals buylded for the poore. Then wer there coleges buylded for the maintenaunce of lernyng." Yea, if they durst they would say, "Then were abbayes & chauntries founded for the realyfe of the pore soules in the bitter payns of Purgatory. Then were our purses filled with the offerynges of the deuout people that vsed to seke the blessed images, and relickes of our Sauior Christ, & of his Blessed Mother Mary with the residue of his saints." If your Highnes would rayse vp but one abbe, chauntry, or pilgremage, you shuld easely perceiue which way thei are bent. We dout not but for these vii. yeres folowyng, masons occupation, with other belongyng to buyldyng, would be the best handy craftes within this your royalme. We praye God their subtill imaginations maye alwaies come to lyghte before thei preuail to the hinderance of Gods veritie. And that it may please hym alwaies to assist your Highnes in the defendyng and settyng furth of the same, to hys glory, and the soul helth of vs, your Highnes most faithful & obedient subiectes. And that you leaue not of, tyll you haue roted out al these sturdy beggers, that the pore members of Christ may haue that porsion to lyue vpon, which was from the beginnynge apointed for them. We meane the x. part of euery mans yerly increase. For though, at the commyng of Christ, and long before, these tenthes were geuen to the pristes of the lawe, yet was it not so from the beginnynge; for at the fyrste, because the world was not so replenished with people, but that euery man was a great possessioner, it was thought good to take of the best of their increase and

THE ORIGIN OF TITHES.

to offer it to the liuyng God in sacrifice, as it appereth by the storie of Abel and Cain. But whan the people grewe to so greate a numbre that euerye man coulde not haue a sufficient porsion to lyue vpon, vnlesse he were able to laboure and tyll the grounde; then was it prouided that euery possessioner shoulde set the tenth of his yearely increase in the porche of hys house, that the lame, blinde, sycke, and diseased, myght be there releued. This order continued tyl the time that Moyses, by the commaundement of God, gaue a lawe to the Israelites, and appoynted that a certayne kynred amongest them, that is, the Leuites, shuld be alwayes theyr priestes, and mynisters of the Tabernacle; vnto whom he appoynted certayne partes of euery sacrifice, that they myght lyue therby. For as yet there was no tenthes to be paied, for then they were in their iorney from Egypt, which iorny continued ful xl. yeres; but after that they wer once settled in the Lande of Promesse, and gathered the fruytes of the grounde, they thought good to geue the tenthes of theyr increase to the priestes that ministred in the Tabernacle, that they myght lyue ther vpon, accordyng to the wordes of the prophet Mal. iii :—" Bring in eueri tenth into my barn, that ther may be meat in my house." But then ther was an other prouysion for the poore, Leui. xxiii. For no man myght lease, rake, or gleane his grounde after he had gathered of his croppe. Noo, they mighte not gather their grapes nor frutes twyse, but must leue the latward fruit, with the scateryng of theyr corne, for the poore to gather, that they myghte haue some relyefe therby; this order continued to the commyng of Chryst. After whose commyng, the Christian sort had all thynges commune, so that no man knewe of any increase, for as much as no man toke anye thynge for hys owne, Actes iiii. But when the numbre of Christians encreased so muche that they possessed hole cyties,

At the first every man offered his sacrifice to God, as we learn by the story of Cain and Abel.

Then Moses gave a law, commanding a certain family to be priests,

who were to receive a part of every sacrifice.

When they were settled in Canaan, tenths of all increase were given to the priests, who ministered in the Tabernacle.

Other provision was made for the poore, so that they might have some share in the produce of the earth.

After Christ, the Christians had all in common.

This did not answer when they increased in number.

countreys, & kyngdomes, it was thought good that euery man should knowe hys owne, to the intent that such as other wyse woulde haue lyued ydly shoulde therby be prouoked to laboure, as apeareth by the rule that Saint Paul gaue to the Tessalonians, ii. Tessaloni. iii.[1], which was thys:—"Who so laboureth not, let hym not eat."

But no tenths were paid to the ministers.

Yet was ther no tenthes payd to the ministers, for Paull wrytinge to the Corinthians, i. Corin. ix., desireth them to be good to such as laboure in the ministration of the Gospell, affirminge that it is but mete that suche as serue the aulter, should haue a liuynge therby; and that it were farre vndesent to musell the oxe that trauaylleth all the daye in treadyng the corne out of the strawe, Deutro. xxv. Which thinge he neded not to haue done, yf the tenthes of ech mans encrease had as than ben geuen to them; for that myght haue sufficed them well ynough (onlesse they had ben as gredye as oure ministres bee, whiche be neuer satisfied[2]).

After this, when the Christian religion was established, and men spent their time over the Scriptures, it was thought good to provide for the poor, by reverting to the old law.

Yet after thys, whan the Christian religion was thorowly stablyshed in many congregations, & many men had laboured ouer the Scriptures, they thoughte good to prouide for the poore impotent creatures accordinge[3] to the example of the auncient fathers of the olde lawe. And bycause they were perswaded that Christ, offering vp him selfe vpon the crosse, had ended all sacrifice, Hebre. x., so that the ministers amonge them neded not to bee pestered with any other thing then preaching, they agreed to adde vnto the preachers an other sort of ministers, which myght supplie the office of holy Steuen, and the other which, in the primatiue church, were appointed to distribute the goodes of the congregation, accordinge as euerye man shoulde stand in neade, Actu. vi. To these men they gaue the tenthe of theyr yerlye encrease, to the intent that they shoulde there vpon

In the apostles' time, deacons were appointed to distribute to the poor, according to their need; and these deacons received the tithes.

---

[1] Orig. iiii.   [2] Orig. satisfieth.
[3] Orig. accordigne.

minister all necessaries, as well to the preachers, as to the poore impotent membres of the churche.

But after that persequution began to sease, & the prechers of the worde of God liued in peace, and that the people were fully bente to learne & followe the doctrine of Christe; they dyd by the preachers, as the Israelites wolde haue doone by Christe, when he had fede so many of them wyth so lytle bread, Iohn vi. They made them theyr rulers, thinkynge that those men which had broughte them out of the darkenes of erroure, and instructed them in the true knowledge of God, coulde best gouerne the publike[1] weale. And woulde walke most vpryghtly in example of lyfe, compellinge the people ther by, to embrace all godlye & honest lyuinge, and to detest and abhore the contrari. This was their intent (most gracious Prince) whan they gaue rule to the preachers of Goddes truth and verite. And in very dede the thinge proued according to their expectation, for a season.

But alasse, after the true shepherdes were departed out of thys lyfe, there entred into the foulde most rauening woulfes, of whom Saint Paule gaue vs warnyng, whan he said "1 know for a certenty, that immediatly after my departinge from you, there shall enter in amonge you certen in sheppes clothing, but inwardly they are rauening wolfes," Act. xx.

The lyke thynge dyd Sainte Peter forsee, when he premonished the elders, that they shold not behaue themselues toward the people, as men hauing dominion ouer them, i. Pe. v.

These hierlinges intended not to maintain & increase the spiritual treasure of the congregation, but to fyl their owne coffers with golde and vayne treasure; to bringe them selues aboue kinges and emperours, yea to be taken for Goddes vicars vpon earthe. And

When persecutions began to cease, and ministers lived in peace, and people began to learn,

they made their ministers rulers, thinking they would walk most uprightly.

This answered for a season.

After these shepherds died

wolves came into the fold,

who only intended to fill their coffers with gold, and to raise themselves above all kings and emperors.

[1] Orig. pubiike.

that they myght the soner bringe this their purpose to passe, they persuaded the people that it should be much more conuenient that they had the tenthes & patrimony of the church (as they cal it) then the deacons, whom the people had elected there vnto. And that it shoulde be more beseaming that the deacones were at theyr fyndinge, then that they shoulde be at the deacons findinge; for they woulde kepe hospitality for the poore, accordinge as the institution of the Apostles was that they should; whiche thynge they could not do onles they had wher withal to maintain it. By these meanes were the people sone persuaded to geue vnto them not onely the tenth, but certein possessions also, to thentent thei might maintayne the more liberal hospitality for the relieue of the pore. This done, all theyr study was to set them selues so hyghe in the conscience of the people, that they shoulde take all theyr traditions to be of no lesse authoritie then the commaundement of God. To do this they could find none so ready a way as to name theyr traditions the lawes of the church. For yf we beleue that Christe is the heade of the churche, and that he is God; then muste we neades graunt that the lawes of the church be Goddes lawes. O diuelish subtiltie, more then serpentical! What subtyl fouler coulde haue diuised a more subtyl trayne to bring the poore, simple byrdes into his nette? Certes, yf al the deuels in hell had ben of theyr counsel (as we thinke they were) they could not haue concluded vpon a more subtil imagination. Now haue they ynough, what neadeth them to seke any further? Now may they commaunde vs to buylde them goodly churches with hyghe steaples, & greate belles to ryng oure pence into theyr purses, when our frendes be dead. Nowe may they make vs beleue that theyr masses be helpful sacrifices, both for the quick and the dead. Nowe must we beleue that the Popes pardons do re-

OF THE CHURCH. 75

lease vs both from payne and faute, but Christ releaseth
the faute only. Now must we beleue they can make of <small>that holy water may become a medicine for body and soul;</small>
two creatures one, that is to say, coniure water and
salte that it be made a medicine both for bodye &
soule ; and of such force that it may be able to roote
out the deuell him self with all hys aungels and minis-
ters. Nowe must we beleue that repentaunce auayleth <small>that repentance avails nothing, unless we confess to a priest.</small>
vs not, onles we declare all our synnes, with the circum-
staunce therof, to one of them, and do such satisfaction
as they shal appoint vs to do. Now can we not denye <small>We must believe that church music is the service of God;</small>
but that the outragiouse belowing of a sorte of[1] sodomi-
ticall buls, myngled with the proud pipyng of organs,
is the seruice of God, and worthy to be preferred before
the redyng and preching of Gods Worde. Now must <small>that He will not hear our prayers unless we are in favour with certain saints.</small>
we beleue that God wyl not heare our praier onles we
be in fauoure with some of the deade saintes which
wyl be our aduocate. Now must we beleue that the <small>We must believe that the gilding of images, the building of religious houses, the giving of ornaments and vestments to the churches, is more acceptable than works of mercy;</small>
making and gilting of ymages, building of abayse,
churches, chauntries, gyldes, hermitages, and gyuinge
of boke, bell, candelsticke, basen, yower, crwetes, pax,
chalyse, corporace, vestimentes, aulter clothes, curtens,
hanginges, towels, torches, tapurs, shepe, sensoures,
pixese, coopes, cannebes, & runnyng on pilgrimage, is
more acceptable to God then the vii. workes of mercy.
Now must we beleue that they can not erre, though <small>we must have faith in the infallibility of the clergy, though they set up the winking rood of Kent.</small>
they set vp the bloude of a ducke to be honored for the
verye bloude of Christe, thoughe they made the Roode
of Kente to wagge hys yies, though they were baudes &
fornicators with the holy whore of Kent. We maye <small>We must think celibacy is right;</small>
not thinke they ought to marye wyues, though we take
them dayly abusinge other mens wyues. We muste <small>we must not say priests are wolves, though we see them buy and sell the congregations of Christ.</small>
not saye that they are rauenynge woulfes, but the true
shepherdes of Christ ; although we see them bothe bye
& sell the congregacions of Christ ; & when they haue
them, loke for nought els but what yearelye rentes may

[1] Orig. af.

7

be clearlye reased therof. Youre Hyghnes knoweth ryghte well what desyre they haue to fead the flocke, for it is not yet many yeares sense youre Hyghnesse, in your hygh Courte and Parliament, was, by theyre negligence, constrayned to establishe a lawe, that, vnder payne of a forfayte, they shoulde preache in euery of theyr paryshes foure tymes in a yeare at the leste, and that none shoulde haue moe benefices then one, whervpon he shoulde be reasident. But here they put your Highnes in mynde of all such chapelyns as do seruice to youre Hyghnes, and to other your nobles of this your realme, besides other, certein graduates ot the vniuersities. Wherevpon it was prouided, by the authorite of the sayd parliament, that euery such chaplayn myght haue many benifices, and be non residence, to lye at the vniuersitie, or els where, at his pleasure, so he wer in any of your nobles seruice. Oh gratious Prince, here are we, your natural, and most obeisant leage people, constrayned to forget (with all humble subiection we speke it) that we are of nature & by the ordinaunce of God your most bounden subiectes, and to cal to remembraunce that by our second byrth we ar your brothers and felowe seruauntes (althoughe in a much inferior ministery) in the houshold of the Lorde our God. Most humble beseking your Highnes to forget also in thys poynte that you are our Leage Lorde and Souerayne, taking our wordes as a token of the feruent desire that we (your most faithful subiects) haue of your solles saluation. Achabe kyng of Israel, whan he intended to make a viage, and to take by force the country and inhabitantes of Ramoth Giliade, he caused hys prophetes, to the nombre of CCCC. false prophetes, to be brought before him, that he might know by them whether the Lord wolde prosper his iorney or not. These false prophetes, standing in the syght of the kynge, & beinge demaunded of him whether he sholde make expedition against Ramoth or not, answered with one voice, "Make expedition, the Lord shal geue it into the handes of the king," iii. Reg. xxii.[1] In lyke maner (most dread Souerayne) your Hyghnes & youre most noble prodicessours, haue alwais *so have you, and your predecessors, and they have told you lies;* consulted a great nombre of false prophetes, which, as Achabes prophetes dyd, prophesied vnto you lies; wringyng & wrestynge the Scriptures to stablishe your Hyghnes in all such thynges as they perseyued you bent vnto. And if at any tyme anye true Micheas haue prophesied vnto you the trueth of Gods Worde, *while he who said the truth was burnt.* one Sedechias or other boxeth him on the cheke that he renneth streight into the fyre. So that hitherto *Your Highness thinks it lawful to give to these flattering priests that which should belong to the poor.* they haue led your Hyghnes in this detestable erroure, that you thyncke it lawfull for you and your nobles, to reward those false flattering Babilon[i]call prophethes wyth that porcion which, by the ordinaunce of God, is dwe to the poore impotent creatures, the lame, blynde, lazer, & sore membres of Christe. We beseke you (most deare Soueraine) euen for the hope you haue in the redemption by Christ, that you call to remembraunce that dreadfull daye, whan your Highnesse *Remember the Day of Judgment,* shall stande before the iudgement seat of God in no more reputation then one of those miserable creatures *when you will stand as he who dies in the streets.* which do nowe daylye dy in the stretes for lack of theyr dwe porsion, wherwith you & your nobles do reward those gnatonical elbowhangers, your chaplaines. Yf theyr ministrie be so necessary to your Highnes that *If your Highness cannot do without these priests, give them livings worthy of their ministration.* you can not lacke them, yet let not the vnsasiable dogges deuour the bread that was prepared for the children; let them be appoynted lyuinges worthy their ministration. What reason is it that a surueyer of *Why should surveyors, alchemists, and goldsmiths have benefices,* bildinges or landes, an alckmist, or a goldsmith, shoulde be rewarded with benefice vpon benefice, which of very reason oughte to be committed to none other but such

---

[1] 1 Kings xxii. in the Authorised Version.

78 PLURALISTS AND NON-RESIDENTS.

which ought only to be given to godly and learned men?

as, through godly lerninge and conuersation, wer able, and would apply them selues, to walke amydes theyr flocke in al godly example and puritie of lyfe? Howe greate a numbre is there of theym that, vnder the name of your chaplynes, may dispend yerly by benefices, some one C., some CC., some CCC., some CCCC., some CCCCC.; yea, some M. markes and more! It is a comone saiyng among vs, your Hyghnes pore commons, that one of your Highnes chapplene, not many yeres synce, vsed, when he lusted to ride a brode for hys repast, to cary wyth hym a scrowle, wherin wer written the names of the parishes wherof he was parson. As it fortuned, in hys iourney he aspied a churche standynge vpon a fayre hyll, pleasauntly beset with groues and playn feldes, the goodly grene medowes liyng beneth by the banckes of a christalline ryuer garnished with wyllouse, poplers, palme trees, and alders, most beautiful to behold. This vigilant pastoure, taken with the syghte of this terestial paradise, sayd vnto a seruaunt of his (the clerke of his signet no doubt it was, for he vsed to cary his masters ryng in his mouth) "Robin," sayd he, "yonder benefice standeth very pleasantly, I would it were myne." The seruaunt aunswered, "Why, syr," quoth he, "it is your owne benefice;" and named the parish. "Is it so?" quoth your chaplen. And with that he pulled out his scroule to se for certentie whether it were so or not.

(Story of the chaplain, who had so many livings

that he didn't know them when he saw them.)

Se (most dread Souerayn) what care they take for the flocke. When they se theyr parysh churches they knowe theim not by the sittuation. If youre Highnes had so manye swyne in youre royalme as you haue men, would ye commyt them to the kepyng & fedyng of such swynherdes as did not know theyr swynsecotes when thei sawe theym? Oh merciful God, how far wide is this our tyme from the primatiue church! Defer not (moost deare Soueraine) the reformation of this

Your Highness would not commit your swine to the keeping of swineherds who did not know the cots when they saw them.

mysse; for the day of the Lord is at hand, and shall come vppon vs as a thefe in the nyght, ii. Peter iii. Disceiue not your selfe through the false gloses of these flatteryng ipocrytes. Turne them out after theyr brethren, the pyed purgatory patriarkes; and restore to the poore members of Christ theyr due portion, which they trusted to haue receiued, when they sawe your Highnes turne out the other sturdy beggers. But alas! thei failed of theyr expectation, and are now in more penurye then euer they were. For, although the sturdy beggers gat all the deuotion of the good charitable people from them, yet had the pore impotent creatures some relefe of theyr scrappes, where as nowe they¹ haue nothyng. Then had they hospitals, and almeshouses to be lodged in, but nowe they lye and storue in the stretes. Then was their number great, but nowe much greater. And no merueil, for ther is in sted of these sturdy beggers, crept in a sturdy sorte of extorsioners. These men cesse not to oppresse vs, your Highnes pore commons, in such sort that many thousandes of vs, which here before lyued honestly vpon our sore labour and trauayl, bryngyng vp our chyldren in the exercise of honest labore, are now constrayned some to begge, some to borowe, and some to robbe & steale, to get food for vs and our poore wiues & chyldren. And that whych is most lyke to growe to inconuenience, we are constrained to suffer our chyldren to spend the flour of theyr youth in idlenes, bringyng them vp other to bear wallettes, other elés, if thei be sturdy, to stuffe prisons, and garnysh galow trees. For such of vs as haue no possessions lefte to vs by oure predicessours and elders departed this lyfe, can nowe get no .ferme, tennement, or cottage, at these mens handes, without we paye vnto theim more then we are able to make. Yea, this was tollerable, so long as, after this extreme exaction, we wer not for the residue of our yeares oppressed with

¹ Orig. thye.

Turn them out after their brethren, and restore to Christ's poor members their due portion.

The poor got relief from the monks,

but now they get nothing; there are no hospitals, and the poor lie and die in the streets.

Extortioners have come in who oppress the poor commons;

who must beg, borrow, or steal.

Our children grow up in idleness,

to stuff prisons,

or garnish the gallows.

We can get no farm, no cottage;

7 ★

much greater rentes then hath of ancient tyme bene paied for the same groundes; for than a man myght within few yeres be able to recouer his fyne, and afterwarde lyue honestly by hys trauel. But now these extorsioners haue so improued theyr landes that they make of xl. s. fyne xl. pounde, and of v. nobles rent v. pound, yea, not suffised with this oppression within theyr owne inheritaunce, they buy at your Highnes hand such abbay landes as you appoint to be sold. And, when they stand ones ful seased therin, they make vs, your pore commons, so in dout of their threatynges, that we dare do none other but bring into their courtes our copies taken of the couentes of the late dissolued monastaries, and confirmed by youre Hygh Court of Parliament, thei make vs beleue that, by the vertue of your Highnes sale, all our former writynges are voyde and of none effect. And that if we wil not take new leases of them, we must then furthwith avoid the groundes, as hauyng therin none entrest. Moreouer, when they can espy no commodious thyng to be boughte at your Highnes hand, thei labour for, and optayne, certayne leases for xxi. yeres, in and vpon such abbay landes as lie commodiously for them. Then do they dashe vs out of countenaunce with your Highnes authorite, makyng vs beleue that, by the vertue of your Highnes leas, our copies are voyde. So that they compell vs to surrender al our former writinges wherby we ought to holde some for ii. and some for iii. lyues, & to take by indenture for xxi. yeres, oueryng both fynes & rentes, beyonde all reason and conscience. This thinge causeth that suche possessioners as here tofore were able and vsed to maintain their owne chyldren, and some of ours, to lernyng and suche other qualites as are necessarye to be had in this your Highnes royalme, are now of necessite compelled to set theyr owne children to labour, and al is lytle inough to pay the lordes rent,

& to take the house anew at the ende of the yeres. So that we your poore commons, which haue no groundes, nor are able to take any at these extorsioners handes, can fynd no way to set our chyldren on worke, no, though we profer them for meat & drynk & poore clothes to couer their bodies. Helpe, merciful Prynce in this extremite; suffer not the hope of so noble a realme vtterly to perysh, through the vnsatiable desyre of the possessioners. Remember that you shal not leaue this kyngedome to a straunger, but to that child of great towardnes our most natural Prince Edward; employ your study to leaue hym a Commune Weale to gouerne, and not an iland of brute beastes, amongest whom the strongest deuour the weaker. Remembre that your office is to defende the innocent & to punysh the oppressar. God hath not suffered al your nobles to distayne their consciences with this most vngodly oppression. If your Highnes would take in hand the redresse of these great oppressions, dout ye not you could lacke no ayde, for he is faythfull that hath promysed to prosper al them that seke his glory and the welth of his pore membres in this church mylitant. Contrariwyse, if you suffre his pore membres to be thus oppressed, loke for none other then the ryghtefull iudgement of God, for your negligence in your offyce and mynistery. For the bloud of all them that, through your negligence shal perysh, shalbe required at your hand. Be merciful therfore to your selfe, & vs your most obeisant subiectes. Indanger not your solle by the sufferyng of vs, your poore commons, to be brought all to the names of beggers & most miserable wreches. Let vs be vnto your Highnes, as the inferiour membres of the bodye to their head. Remembre that your hore heares are a token that nature maketh hast to absolue the course of your lyfe; preuente the subtile imaginations of them that galpe, and loke after the crowne of

Help us in our extremity, and do not suffer the hope of the realm to perish!

Study to leave your son, Prince Edward, a Commonwealth, not an island of beasts.

Remember you are the defender of the innocent, and the punisher of the oppressor.

If you will redress our grievances you are sure of aid;

if not, the blood of those who die by your negligence will be required at your hands.

Remember your hoar hairs are a token that your life must soon end, and prevent the imaginations of

SUPPLICATION. G

SIMONY, USURY, AND VICE.

[margin: such as gape for your death.]

this realme after your daies. For what greater hope can thei haue as concerning that[1] detestable and deuylysh imagination, then that they might wynne the hertes of vs, your Hyghnes commons, by the deliueryng vs from the captiuite and mysery that we are in?

[margin: We pray you may live to see the confusion of all such traitors,]

We beseke God, your Highnes maye lyue to put awaye al such occasions, and to se the confusion of all suche trayterous hertes; and that youre Grace may se that worthy Prynce Edward able to gouerne and defend this your realme, vanquishyng all his enemyse, bothe far

[margin: and see your son able to govern the realm.]

and nere, as your Highnes, by the ayde of Almightie God, hath done hitherto. Defer not, most dread Souerayne Lorde, the reformation of these so great enormities; for the wound is euen vnto death, if it continue anye whyle lenger. A prynce welbeloued of his people is muche more ryche then he that hath houses full of gold. And yet is he much more ryche that is beloued of God. For if God bee on your part, who can preuayle agaynst your Hyghnes? By thys we meane the great and

[margin: Vice is rampant in the land.]

myghtie abhomination of vyce, that nowe rayneth within this your Highnesse realme this day. For hordome is more estemed then wedlocke, although not vniuersally, yet amongest a great numbre of lycensious persons.

[margin: Simony has lost its name, and usury is lawful gain. Unless these things be redressed, they will bring the wrath of God upon us. By our example we are worse than Jews or Mahometans.]

Simoni hath lost hys name, and vsery is lawfull gaynes.

These thinges, onlesse they be redressed, wyl bringe the ire of God vpon the realme. For what doth it lesse then declare vs to be cleane fallen from the doctrine of Christ, who taught vs to lende, lokinge to haue no gayne therby? What example of lyfe is in vs this daye to declare, that we rather bee the people of God then the Iewes or Maometanse? Certes (most renomed Prince) none but that we confesse hym to be God. And that were sufficient, yf our deedes dyd not denye him. Yf the rulers haue geuen the occasion of these thynges, alas for them; they had ben better to haue had mylstones hanged about theyr neckes, and haue

[1] Orig. than

ben cast into the sea. But if the people haue taken it of them selues, and be not punished of the rulers, but be permitted frelye to vse it; the blud of them that perish shalbe requered at the watchmans hand, Ezechi. xxxiii. Thus princes are punished when the people offende. But now (most deare Souerayne) your Highnes may in this matter try your prelates whether they be of God or nat; for yf they were of God, they woulde, accordinge to the wordes of the prophet, neuer sease, but openly and with a criynge voyce, declare vnto the people theyr faultes, Esai. lviii, and not be hushed wyth an acte in parliament; for that declareth them to be the setters forthe of mans tradicyons and not of Godes lawes, so that this saying of our Sauiour Christ is verifyed in them:—"This people honoreth me with theyr lyppes, but their herte is fare from me: they teache the doctrines and commaundementes of men," Math. xv. But here they thynke to stop oure mouthes wyth the feare of youre Highnesse displeasure; they say youre Highnes lawes are Godes lawes, & that we are as moch bounde to obserue them as the lawe of God geuen by Moyses. Trueth it is (most deare Lorde), that we are bounde by the commaundement of God, to obey your Hyghnesse, & all youre lawes set forth, by your Hygh Court of Parliament, but yf they dissent from or be contrary to anye one iote of the Scripture, we muste, with Ihon & Peter, say, Actu. iiii, "Iudge you whether it be better for vs to obeye God or man." We speake not this because we think by this, that we may rebel agaynst you, our naturall Prince. But that yf youre Hyghnes would enforce vs by a law to do any thing contrary to that God hath commaunded vs, that then we ought manfully to cleaue to the truth of Godes word, boldly confessing the truth therof, fearing nothing the death of this body; and yet moost humble submittinge oure selues vnto you, redy to abyde and pacientlye to suffer what kynde of torment so euer

If the prelates are of God,

they will tell the people of their faults.

They tell us we must keep the laws of the king as we would keep the laws of God.

True; but if they dissent from God's laws,

we must act as John and Peter did.

We don't say this because we think we may rebel, but if you would enforce us to anything contrary to God's law,

should be leyd vpon vs, knowing for certenty that we are happy when we suffer persecution for the truthes sake, and that he is faythfull that hath promessed to be reuenged of oure iniuries. But these dombe dogges haue lerned to faine vpon them that vse to bringe them bread, and to bee wonderful hasty when they be mantayned and cherished ; but yf they be but ones byde cowche, they know their liripope so well that they draw the tayle betwine the legges, and gette them selues streyght to the kennell. And then come who so wyll, and do what they wyll, these dogges wyll stere no more tyll they heare theyr maister saye, "hye cut and longe tayle." So frayd they are of stripes, and leste they shoulde be tyde vp so short that they myght not raynge a brode and wory now and than a simple lambe or two. Before it was passed by Acte of Parliament that men myghte take x. li. by yeare for an hondreth pound lone, how vehement were they in the matter ? All theyr sermons were lytle other then inuectiues agaynst vsery. Then they could alleage both Christ and the Psalmist to proue that Christen men ought to lende what they may spare, & to loke for no gaynes therof. But nowe they do not onlye holde them selues styll as concernynge thys matter, but also they endeuoure to imitat, yea, and to passe the example of the extorsyoners and vserers. For euen the laste yeare they opteyned by theyr importune sute, a graunte whych, yf it be not reuoked, wyll in continuaunce of tyme be the greateste impouirishment of vs your poore commons (and chyfly in the citie of London) that euer chanced sence the fyrst beginnyng therof. They haue obtayned, and it is enacted, that euery man wythin the sayd cytie; shall yearly pay vnto them accordynge to the rentes they are charged wyth xvi. d. ob. of euery x. s. So that yf the lordes of the groundes do double & triple the rentes (as they do in dead) then most the pore tenantes paye also double & triple tenthes as dwe encrease of their riches: this is not vnlyke vnto that which is practised in the contry amongest vs your Highnes poore commones. For when it hath pleased God to punish vs with the rot of our shepe, so that perhappes some one of vs hathe hylded C. shepe, then haue some of the persons constrayned vs to geue them x. of the felles, for they cal it increase so longe as we sell them. And therfore must they (as Godes debities) take the tenth therof. Haue compassion vpon vs (most gracius Soueraine); suffer not these vnsatiable dogges thus to eat vs out of al that we haue; considre that it is against al reason & conscience, that we, your pore commones, should be thus oppressed; that where the landlorde taketh of vs duble & triple rent, that then we shall pay also to the person duble or triple tenthes. But see (moost dere Souerayne) howe craftely they haue wroughte thys feate; they requyre not the tenthes of the lande lordes that haue the increase, but of the tenauntes, whych of necessitye are constrayned to pay to the lordes theyr askynge, other elles to be without dwellinge places. They know right well that yf they shoulde haue matched them selues with the landelordes, they happelye shoulde haue bene to weake for them at the lengthe. But they were in good hope that we (your poore commons) shoulde neuer be able to stande in theyre handes, as in verye deed we shall not onles your Hyghnes wyll voultsafe to take our cause in hand; for yf we haue not wherwith to pay them, they mai, by the vertue of the acte distresse suche implementes as they shal fynde in our houses. They know our conditions of olde, sence they toke theyre mortuaries. We had rather, in maner, famysh oure selues for lack of fode, and to make right harde shyft besydes, then that we woulde be troubled for anye suche thyng. And doutlesse (most renomed Prince) yf the oppression were not

It is as bad in the country.

If 100 sheep die of rot, the parsons compel us to give them 10 of the skins: they call it all increase.

Don't let us be thus oppressed, to pay double or triple tenths, on double or triple rents.

We cannot stand against the priests, unless you take our cause in hand.

We would rather starve than trouble your Highness,

and if the oppression had

to moch beyond all reason and conscience, we woulde neuer haue troubled youre Highnes with all. Yea, yf there were any hope that they would be satisfied by this, we woulde rather fast iii. dayes euery weake, then we woulde seame to be slack in doyng all such thynges as the lawe byndethe vs to. But we se daylye so great increase of theyre vnsatiable desire, that we fear lest in processe of time they wil make vs all begge an[d] brynge to them all that we can gette. It is no rare thinge to se the poore impotent creatures begge at Easter to pay for the Sacrament when they receaue it. And it is no lesse commune to se men begge for such dead corpses as haue nothinge to paye the pristes duitie.[1] Yea it is not longe sence there was in your Highnes cytie of London a dead corps brought to the church to be buryed, beyng so poore that it was naked wythout any cloth to couer it. But these charitable men, whiche teache vs that [it] is one of the workes of mercy to bury the dead, woulde not take the paynes to bury the dead corps, onlesse they had theyr dutye, as they call it. In fyne, they caused the dead corps to be caryed into the strete agayne, and there to remayne tyll the poore people, whych dwelled in the place where the poore creature dyed, had begged so moch as the pristes call theyr dwe. O mercifull Lord, who can be able worthily to lament the miserable estate of thys tyme? When those men whiche in all thynge professe to be the light of the worlde, the teachers of the ignoraunte, & the leaders of the blynd, are so fare withoute mercy (whyche Christe preferred before sacrifice) that they wyl not do so moch as wast a lytle of theyr breathe in readinge ouer a fewe psalmes at the buryall of one of the poore membres of Christ, onlesse they haue money for theyr laboure! And whan those persons whom the other, called spiritual, do compt but as brute beastes, callynge them temporall, shall showe more mercy, the badge of

[1] Orig. diuitie.

the Christian souldiers, towardes the poore membres of Christ, then they which glory to be the true prophetes of Christ, and successoures of the Apostles! Yea, when those paynted sepulcres be so merciles that they pitie not them, whom the verye infidelles woulde pitie! Wher is theyr so litle mercy showed as amongest them? In so much that theyr couetouse is growne into this prouerbe, "No peny, no pater noster." For they wyl not do that thyng whych euery Christian is bounde to do for other, onles they may be waged for money; they wedde and bury, and synge ful mery, but all for money. If your Highnes would call a compt of them, and cause them to showe the bokes of the names of them that haue ben buryed & maried with in thys yeare, conferringe that numbre wyth the summe of money they take for euery such burial & mariage, you should easily perseaue howe lytle neade they haue to oppresse vs with double & triple tenthes. Iudge then (most victoryouse Prince) what an vnresonable summe the whole & grosse summe of these enhanced tenthes wyth other theyr pettyt bryburrye, draweth to. They receaue of euery hondreth li. xiii. li. xv. s., & of the thousande, one hundreth, and xxxvii. li. x. s. Then may youre Highnes soone be certifyed what they receyue of the whole rentes of the citie. No doute (gracyouse Prynce) they receyue of vs yearely moore then your Hyghnes dyd at anye tyme whan you were besette on euery syde wyth mortall enemyes. And yet theyr conscience woulde serue them wel ynowgh to take three tymes as moche as they do, yf your Hyghnes woulde suffer them. For they vse to saye that, for as moche as it is establyshed by a lawe, they may, wyth good conscience, take it yf it were more. Yea yf your Hyghnes woulde suffer them, theyr conscience woulde serue them to lye wyth our wiues euery tenthe nyghte, other els to haue euerye tenthe wyfe in the paryshe at theyre

Their covetousness has grown into a proverb:

"No penny, no pater noster."

The fees they receive for marriages and burials render tithes unnecessary.

Of every £100, they receive £13 15s.

They receive more than your Highness did when beset by mortal enemies; yet they wish for more.

They would tithe our wives, if they were permitted.

TENTHS AND SEVENTHS.

Before long they will endeavour to make your Highness pay tithes;

pleasure. But oure trust is that your Hyghnesse wyll tye them shorter, and to saye the truethe it is tyme; for yf you suffer them a whyle they wyll attempt to make your Highnes pay the tenthes vnto them as longe as they haue payed them to you. For they haue already soughte oute our ware houses, store houses, stables,

as they compel us, not only to pay them, but the seventh penny of our rents also.

wharffes, and barnes, causynge vs to paye, not onely the tenthe for that we neuer payd before; but also the vii. peny of the whole rentes, raised throughout the whole cytie. Who can iudge other therfore (moost dreade

They will require your Highness to pay the tenth of the spoils of your enemies, as Melchisedec did to Abraham.

Souerayne) but that they wold, yf thei wist how, cause your Highnes to pay vnto them not only the tenth of your yerely reuenues, but also the tenthe peny of all such spoiles as youre Highnes shall take in warres; for they carp moch vpon Abrahams geuinge of the tenth of his spoile to Melchisedech. Wherfor most merciful Prince, consider with mercy this pitiful complaint of vs your most faithful subiects, deliuering vs from the mouthes of these vnsaciable beastes, which do daylye employ them selues to deuoure vs, our wyues and childerne, euen as we were fode prepared for them to de-

Let Paul's order take effect, and allow none to eat who will not work.

uoure. Let the order that Paule toke withe the faythfull of the primatiue church, take effect in these our days, the last days of this miserable world. Let none eat that laboureth not, ii. Thessa. iii.[1] Let them also that be called to be preachers, haue the rewarde of preachers; ouerlode them not with the possessions & ryches of this world, for the cares therof do choke the worde. Let not eche rauenynge woulfe that commeth wyth a shepehoke in hys hande be receued as a shep-

Let not Christ's lambs be given into the care of wolves,

herde. Let not the simple lambes of Christ be committed to the tuition of these so raueninge woulfes. Let not the porcion of the poore be committed to them that distribute not, but rather gather and heape vp, coumptynge all fyshe that cometh to the net. Let the

[1] Orig. iiii.

worthy prophetes that walke diligently in theyr vocacion, be called to the gouernance of the spiritual flocke of Christ, and let them be repelled that come vncalled, we meane suche as ·sue to beare the name of youre Hyghnesse chaplaynes, onelye because they trust to optayne therby lordlyck liuinges out of the porsion of the poore. Take pity (mooste mercifull Prince) vpon vs youre poore, and faythful leage people; take pitty vppon youre owne soule, which shall at the laste daye be charged wyth all abuses that your Hyghnes suffereth frely to raygne. Beleue not those gnatonicall adherentes that wyll not sticke[1] to affirme and denye, so that they may trust to please you therby. Let them not perswade your Highnes that al is good that is concluded in your Hygh Court of Parliament. Remembre, O, howe they ledde your Hyghnes whan you sent forthe your letters vnder your broode seale, streyghtly commaundinge euery and singuler your Highnes subiectes, vnder payne of youre Highnes displeasure, to ayde, supporte, and forther all and singular prockters & pardoners. Remembre in what case they had brought iour Highnes whan you thought it godlynes to viset in your owne parson the graues, images, & relickes of dead saintes, doing to them diuine honour & reuerence. Let them not perswade you that God is or can be better serued in the Latine tong then in the Englysh; consider what great folly Saynte Paull counteth it for men to pray, which is to talke wyth almighty God, in a tong they vnderstand not, i. Corin. xiiii. Yea and how moch greater folly it is to thyncke holynes in hearynge a tale told in a straunge tong. Your Hyghnes commaunded that none should receaue the Sacrament at Easter,[2] but such as coulde and dyd vse the Lordes prayer wyth the articles of the fayth in the Englysh tong. But they byd vs vse that which is most ready to vs.

[1] Orig. stickt.   [2] Orig. Erster.

SERVICES IN LATIN.

<small>They baptize in Latin, making us say 'Volo' and 'Credo,' when we don't know what is asked of us, and know not what we profess.</small>

They baptyse oure chylderne in the Latyne tong, beding vs say, 'Volo,' and 'Credo,' whan we know not what it is that they demande of vs. By this meane is it broughte to passe that we know not what we professe in our baptisme, but superstitiously we think that the holynes of the wordes whych sound so straungly in oure eares, & of the water that is so oft crossed is the doyng of all the matter. Yea we thyncke that yf our chyl-

<small>If a child receives any hurt we blame the priest, and say that member was not well christened,</small>

dren be well plunged in the founte they shalbe healthfull in all theyr lims euer after, but yf they, by any misaduenture, receyue any hurte in any of theyr membres, incontinent we ley the faute in the prist, sayinge, that member was not wel christened. Oh mercifull God, what hert can be able worthely to lament this more then Iewdaical superstition? The

<small>applying that which is spiritual wholly to the flesh.</small>

thing that is mere spirituall, we applye whollye to the flesh. Was there euer any vayne ydolatours that woulde honour theyr goddes in a language they vnderstode not? Were the monckes, friers, and chanons, wyth other superstitious religions, professed in a

<small>The oath of obedience to your Majesty is in English, that we may know what is our duty.</small>

straunge tong? Is not the othe of obeysaunce that we your leage people take vnto you, ministred in the English tonge? And for what other purpose but that we may therby knowe our mooste bounden deuitie toward you oure naturall Prince and Leage Lorde? Is

<small>Why then should not the oath which we take to God be in a language which we can understand?</small>

it then beseamyng that we, takynge an othe of obeysaunce to the Kynge of all kynges, the God of all the world, and Maker therof, shulde not know what is demaunded of vs nor what we answere agayne? Yf we hold vs styll as concerning thys more then hell darkenesse, the very stones of your pallayce woulde make exclamation. Preuent therfore, most gracious Prince, the yre of God whiche hangeth ouer thys your royalme. Remember that his long sufferance shalbe recompensed wyth the extremitie of the punyshment. Wherfore,

<small>We pray God to preserve your</small>

most worthy Prince, we humbly beseke oure heauenly

Father, the Geuear of al goodnes, euen for the Lord <small>Highnees, giving you grace to walk circumspectly,</small>
Iesu Christes sake oure Sauyoure and Redeamer, that
he preserue you alwayes, geuinge you grace to walke
circumspectly in your vocation and ministery, that, at <small>and bring you to heauen at last.</small>
the last day, you may receaue the incorruptible crowne
of glory, and reigne with our Elder Brother the fyrst
begotten Sonne of God the Father Almighty; to whom
wyth the Holy Goost be all honore and glory
for euer and euer. All true
Englysh hertes saye,
Amen.

Pealme. xl.[1]

¶ Happy is the man that pitieth the poore: for in
tyme of trouble the Lord shal deliuer hym.

THus haue we (your moost obeisant subiectes) de- <small>Thus haue we declared our wishes for your success in this life and in the next.</small>
clared the feruent desire we haue not only of your
prosperous succes in the affaires of this life, but also of
your eternal reign with the Lord Iesu in the celestial
kingdom, of whose fayth ye are, in earth, Defender,
and of the faythfull congregacion, in thys lytle angle
of the earth congregate, the Supreme Heade immediatlye
nexte vnto him, by whose mighty hand you haue <small>By God's hand you have vanquished all the enemies</small>
hytherto vanquished, not onely the externe enemies of
this moost noble royalme, but all such as haue most
dyuilyshly ymagined, conspired, & attempted treason
against youre Hyghnes, theyr moost naturall Leage
Lord and Gouernour. What histories should we reade
to know of so many and so daungerous conspirations, <small>who have conspired against you.</small>
so wonderfully detect & auoyded? Who myghte so
sone haue wrought the most detestable purpose of
treason, as she that slept in your bosom? What mighty
princes haue ben betrayed by them that they haue
loued aboue all creatures? And howe wonderfullye,
euen at the verye poynt,[2] and in the time of most

[1] xli. in Au. Ver.   [2] Orig. yoynt.

daunger, hath the myghtye hande of the Lorde delyuered you? Besydes this, that moost abominable ydoll of Rome, which sate so hygh not only in the consciences of vs your most bounden subiectes & poore commones but also your nobles (euen from the highest to the lowest) were all hys faythfull adherentes; in so moche that som of them would not styck to sheade the best bloude of theyr bodyes in hys quarel. And yet how wonderfully hath the Lord our God, made him iour fote stole? Reioise (deare Souerayne) reioyce. The Lord is your right hande, he hath found you faythful in a lytle, & shall ordeyne you ouer moch more. Onely beware that you, puttyng your hande to the ploughe, do not loke backwarde. Go forthe manfully to conquere, and turne not agayne tyll you haue purged this vineyard of the Lorde, so that there remayne not one lytle impe besydes those that our Heauenly Father hath planted. Let not that noble Prince Edwarde be oppressed in the dayes of hys youth, with the combrouse weadynge oute of suche rotton and fruyteles trees, lest perchaunce they take deaper roote then that his tender youthe may be able to moue. Forget not your owne youth, when these adulterine trees were to stronge for you. Thynke not but that you shall leaue behynd you a great nombre that wolde be glad to se the old stompes of these fruitles trees sprynge agayne. The Lord bringe them all to confusion, geuyng your Highnes long lyfe, with assistence of hys grace, to performe that whyche you haue begonne. The wysdom of the Lorde oure God leade you into all trueth. Amen.

¶ Your moste faythfull and
obeysaunt subiectes, the Pore
Commones of the Royalme
of Englande.

Anno. M. ccccc. xlvi.

¶ Certayne

causes gathered together, wherin is shewed the decaye of England, only by the great multitude of shepe, to the vtter decay of houshold keping, mayntenaunce of men, dearth of corne, and other notable dyscommodityes approued by syxe olde Prouerbes.

Prouer. 20

A Kyng that sitteth in iudgement, and loketh well about him, dryueth away all euell.

[*The title of the Lambeth copy had* Causes, onely, multytude, housholde kepyng, Kynge, euyll.]

To the Kynges moste honorable Counsell, and the Lordes of the Parlayment house.

THe fyrst Article & poynt, as we do thynke, it is[1] great pyttye (so the will of God it were) that there is not[2] corne ynough within this Realme of Englande, at all tymes necessary to certyfy & suffyce the Kynges subiectes for the space of one yere, two, or thre, yf there were no corne sowen in this Realme by the sayde space. *It is a pity there is not corn enough in England to last 1, 2, or 3 years, if there were none sown during the same period.*

We do saye that *the* Kinges Maiestie, mercifully hearing the peticion of these his graces poore subiectes, maye at al tymes remedy it, when it shall *please hys Maiestie, being for a common wealth for his graces subiectes, & to the greate encrease of this noble realme of England. *The king can remedy the matter when it shall please him [* sign. A .ij.] so to do.*

We saye, as reason doeth leade vs, *that* shepe & shepemasters, doeth cause skantyte of corne, whiche we do thynke[3] it maye be well approued, by reason of six prouerbes; for & yf all our lyuynges, and all our commodities, were diuyded in partes, by reason of *the* same syx prouerbes, we that be *the* Kynges Maiestyes poore subiectes, do lose syx of our commodityes, then haue we thre losses, whiche make nyne; by reason of the same thre losses, we, the Kynges Magestyes[4] subiectes, do lose *the* third part of our lyuinge, then haue we the tenth part, which we cal a remedy, beseching your noble grace, to remedye when your Maiestye shall please. *Sheep and sheepmasters cause scarcity of corn, as six proverbs will prove. For if all our livings were divided into parts we lose 6 commodities, have 3 losses, and the tenth part which is called a remedy.*

---

[1] is it—C(ambridge copy).   [2] no—C.
[3] thincke—Lambeth copy; and with a *c* elsewhere.
[4] mayestyes—C.

8 ★

1ˢᵀ PROVERB. NO STORE SET BY TILLAGE.

Concerning the first proverb.

As touchyng the fyrste prouerbe of the syx, we do thynke

The more shepe, the dearer is the woll.
The more shepe, the dearer is the motton.
The more shepe, the dearer is the beffe.
The more shepe, the dearer is the corne.
The more shepe, the skanter is the whit meate.

[* sign. A .iij.] The more shepe, the fewer egges for a peny.*

In the 1st proverb the complaint is from Oxfordshire, Bucks, and Northampton-shire.

In *t*he fyrst prouerbe, *t*he more shepe, the dearer is the woll. Our complaynt is for Oxford-shyre, Buckyngham-shyre, & Northampton-shyre ; and as for all other shyres, we refer it to the playntyues[1].

We desire you to pardon our ignorance, but to consider what we advance, seeing it is done for the good of the realm.

We shal desyre you, and al other that reade and se the true ententes & meanynges of this our doinges, to pardon our ignoraunce ; yet not withstandyng, we desyre you sumwhat to attender the premisses, seinge it is done, and put forth, for the commoditye of *t*he Kinges Magesties realme, and for the welth of his graces poore subiectes.

In these 3 counties are many landowners

In the sayde Oxford-shyre, Buckyngham-shyre, & Northhampton-shyre, there be many men of worshyp dwellyng within the sayde thre shyres, and hath great landes to lyue vpon, the which we praye to God to geu̇e them ioye of, and well to occupye it. Many of these

who set no store by tillage,

worshipful men, sette no store, nor pryse, vpon the mayntenaunce of tyllage of theyr landes, as before tyme

nor yet by breeding and feeding cattle,

hath been vsed, neyther breadyng nor feadynge of catle, but many of them doeth kepe the most substaunce of theyr landes in theyr owne handes[2]. And where

but stock their land with sheep.

tillage was wont to be, nowe is it stored wyth greate vmberment of shepe : & they that haue great vmberment of shepe, muste nedes haue greate store of woll,

[† sign. A .iiij.] and we cannot thynke †who shulde make the pryse of woll, but those *t*hat haue great plentye of shepe. And we do partly knowe that there be some dwellynge

[1] playntynes—C. [2] L(ambeth copy) repeats *des* by mistake.

within these thre shyres, rather then they wyll sell theyr woll at a lowe pryse, they will kepe it a yere or twayne, and all to make it deare, and to kepe it a deare pryse. And by this meanes *the* fyrst prouerbe to be true : The more shepe, the dearer is the woll. *Rather than sell wool at a low price they keep it to make it dear. So the 1st proverb is true.*

In the seconde prouerbe, as we do thynke : The more shepe, the dearer is *the* moton. *The 2nd proverb: The more sheep, the dearer the mutton.*

As by reason, the most substaunce of our feadynge was wont to be on beffe, and now it is on motton. And so many mouthes goith to motton, whiche causeth motton to be deare. *We used to feed beef, now it is mutton, and so many eat it that it is dear.*

In the third prouerbe, as we do thinke : The more shepe, the dearer is the beffe. *The 3rd proverb: The more sheep, the dearer the beef.*

As by reason that breding and fedyng, is not set by as it hath bene in tymes past; and where as shepe is kepte vpon the pasture groundes where breadyng & fedinge of beffes was wont to be kept[1], And now there is nothyng kept there but motton. *Beef used to be fed, now there is nothing but mutton.*

The fourth prouerbe : The more shepe, the dearer is the corne. *The 4th proverb: The more sheep, the dearer the corn.*

By reason tyllage is *not vsed, occupyed, and mainteyned as it hath bene before tyme, but shepe kept vpon the grounde, where tyllage was wont to be kept and mainteyned. *[* A 5] Tillage is not now used, but sheep are kept on the ground.*

The .v. prouerbe : The more shepe, the skanter is the weyte meate. *The 5th proverb: The more sheep, the scanter the white meat.*

By reason tyllage is[2] not vsed, occupyed, and maynteyned, nother mayntenaunce of houses and hospitalytye, where as catle was wont to be fede and brede; by reason of kepyng of catle, shulde increase whyt meate; and now there is nothyng kept there but only shepe. *Where cattle were fed, white meat was increased.*

The syxte prouerbe : The more shepe, the fewer egges for a peny. *The 6th proverb: The more sheep, the fewer eggs for a penny.*

---

[1] The Cambridge copy repeats '& where as shepe is kept vpon the pasture groundes, where bredyng and fedynge was wont to be kept.'   [2] it—L.

NINE LOSSES. THE PRODUCE OF ONE PLOW.

Poultry was bred by cottagers: now there is nothing but sheep.

By reason cottages go downe in the contre, where as pultrye was wont to be breade and fedde, nowe there is nothyng kept there but shepe, which cause the egges to be solde for fower a penny.

Thus the six proverbs are true.

Thus be the syx prouerbes true, as we do thynke, desyrynge you to geue hearynge vnto them, and that it may be wel amended, for the common welthe of the Kynges poore subiectes.

Three losses which make nine.

Then haue we thre losses, that maketh nyne.

1. Fewer plows by forty in Oxfordshire.

The fyrst losse, as we do thinke, there is not so many plowes vsed, occupied and mainteyned within Oxforthshyre as was in Kynge Henry the Seuenth tyme, and sens hys fyrste comming there lacketh xl.

Each plow kept six persons.

plowes, euery plough was able to kepe vi. persons, downe lyinge and vprisynge in hys house, the whiche draweth to twelf score persons in Oxfordshyre.

And where *tha*t the sayde twelf score persons were wont to haue meate, drynke, rayment and wages, payinge skot and lot to God & to our Kyng, now there is nothyng kept there, but onlye shepe. Now these twelfscore persons had nede to haue liuing:—whether shal they go? into Northhamptonshyre? and there is also the lyuinge of twelef score persons loste: whether shall then they goo? foorth from shyre to shyre, and to be scathered thus abrode, within *th*e Kynges maiestyes Realme, where it shall please Almighty God; and for lacke of maisters, by compulsion dryuen, some of them to begge, and some to steale.

Now there is nothing but sheep.

These 240 persons must live—where shall they go?

Some of these are driven to beg, some to steal.

2. Besides keeping 6 persons, every plow gives 30 quarters of grain a year to sell, and 40 plows, each yielding 30 quarters, make 1200 quarters in each county.

The seconde losse, as we do thinke: That there is neuer a plough of the .xl. plowes, but he is able to tyll and plowe to certifye syx persons, and euery ploughe to sell .xxx. quarters of grayne by the yeare, or els he can full yll paye, syx, seuen, eyght poundt by the yeare. xl plowes, .xxx. quarters euery ploughe, draweth to two[1]

---

[1] This " two hundreth " must mean twelve hundred : 40 × 30 = 1200.

hundreth quarters in Buckingham shyre, two hundreth quarters in Oxfordeshyre, & two .cc. quarters in Northampton shyre, & so forth from shyre to shyre in certayne shyres within the Kinges Maiesties Realme of Englande. what shall the twelf two hundreth quarters of corne do in Oxforthshyre ? we do thynke it wyll mainteyne the Kynges markettes, and sustayne the Kynges subiectes; and lykewyse in Buckyngham shyre, & also in Northampton shyre and so from shyre to shyre, in certayne shyres wythin the Kynges Magesties Realme. Furthermore it is to be consydered what thys twelf hundreth quarters of corne is able to do within Oxfordshyre, it is able to certifye & suffyce xv. score people by the yeare, bread and drynke, & allowe to euery person ij. quarters of weate, and two quarters of malt, by the yere; where as in the fyrst the hole lyuinge of twelf score persons, meate, & drynke, and rayment, vpryʀ-yng & downe lyinge, payinge skot and lot to our God, and to our Kyng. And the seconde losse, bread and drynke for .xv score persons by the yeare, whiche the hole nombre draweth to .v. hundreth and .xl. persons in Oxforth shyre; and¹ so in Buckyngham shyre, & so lykewyse in Northampton shyre, and so forth from shyre to shyre wythin the Kynges Maiestyes Realme.

<small>These 1200 quarters of corn</small>

<small>would keep 300 persons a year.</small>

<small>The whole second loss in Oxfordshire draws near 540 persons.</small>

And yf it be as we do think, that there be .iiij. score plowes in euery one of these shires les then there was, then is there the lyuyng lost of a thousand & iiij. score persons in euerye one of these foresayde shyres. Thys is the seconde losse, as we do thynke, and call for remedy for it.

<small>It is thought there are 80 plows lost in each shire.</small>

The thirde losse, as we do thinke : We do lose in the sayd thre shyres kepynge of houshold and hospitalitye, & maintayning of tyllage and houshold kepyng; we do lacke corne, and also lese our cattell ; for where any housholde is kept, there is kept kyne

<small>3. The third loss is in households, hospitality, and tillage.</small>

<small>Every house kept kine,</small>

¹ C omits 'and'.

and calues; and of oure kine there commeth mylke, butter and chease; and all this doeth sustayne the Kynges Mayesties subiectes; and for thys we haue nothynge but shepe.

<small>hogs, poultry, and other commodities,</small>

And furthermore, where housholdes be kept, there is hogges, pygges, and bakon, capons, hennes, duckes, egges, frute, and many other commodityes, that is necessary & nedefull to be had for the maintenaunce and lyuinge of the Kynges Maiesties poore subiectes to lyue by; and for that we haue nothyng but shepe. This is the thyrd losse.

<small>for which we have only sheep.</small>

<small>The 10th point, the Remedy.</small>

The .x. is, which we do cal for remedy, and we desyre of God and the Kynges Maiestye, yf it shal please his Highnes to be so good & gracyous vnto his poore subiectes, that there might be in euery shyre & hundred, as many plowes vsed, occupyed, and maynteyned, *as many housholds kept, as was by king Henry the Seuenth tyme, fyrst commynge. And then vnfayned, as we do thynke, we sholde haue corne ynough, cattell ynough, and shepe ynough; then wil shepe and woll be in more mens handes; we shall haue also white meate ynough, and all thynges necessary. And thus Iesu preserue oure dreade soueraingne Lorde and Kynge!

<small>A hundred times as many plows should be kept, and as many [* sign. B] households as in Henry VII's time, then there would be enough.</small>

<small>Two more losses.</small>

<small>1. In Households, Tillage, and Shooters.</small>

<small>Shepherds are but ill archers.</small>

<small>2. The king loses in provisions for his household,</small>

<small>to the amount of 5000 marks a year.</small>

As we do thynke, we haue two losses more that we haue not spoken: The firste losse is for lacke of houshold kepynge & mayntenaunce of tyllage. It is great decay to artyllary: for that do we reken that shepeherdes be but yll artchers. And as we do further thinke, it leseth the kings Maiesty in prouision for his noble housholdes, that is to saye, in wheat, malt, benes, mottons, veles, hay and otes, and pultry, & all maner suche prouisions that belongeth to hys Maiestyes housholde, as we do thynke, v. thousande markes by the yeare with the left. In a trial as we do thynke, yf it shuld please the Kynges Maiesties offycers to call in hys graces purueyers, & examyne them where they haue had within their tyme for his graces prouisions of his warres, & for his Maiestyes housholde, where as there is nowe nothyng to be gotten: for they that kepe the sayde landes, hath put the foresayde landes to pastures, *themself byeth all maner of grayne & corne to kepe theyr housholde with all.

<small>Those who keep the lands, and have put them to pasture, [* sign. B. ij.] buy grain to keep their household.</small>

Furthermore, yf it shall please the Kinges Highnes, and hys noble counsell, for to haue a further tryall of thys matter, and to assure it to be true, take al craftes men dwelling in cyties & townes, daye laborers that laboreth by water or by lande, cottygers & other housholders, refusyng none, but only them that hath al this aboundaunce, that is to saye, shepe or wollmasters, and inclosers, the lamentacions of the Kinges Maiestyes subiectes will make any true herted body to seke & call for remedy, whiche we beseche the Lorde to amende. Amen.

<small>Take all craftsmen, and all labourers, and their lamentation will make a true man call for remedy.</small>

Furthermore, as we do thinke, this Realme doeth decaye by thys meanes: It is to vnderstande and knowen, that there is in England, townes and villages to the nomber of fifty thousand & vpward, & for euery towne and vyllage,—take them one with an other throughout all,—there is one plowe decayed sens the fyrste yeare of the raigne of kynge Henry the Seueuth. And in som townes and vyllages all the hole towne decayed sens that time; and yf there be for euery towne and village one plough decayed, sens the first yeare of the raygne of kyng Henry the Seuenth, then is there decayed .l. thousande plowes and vpwarde.

<small>In each of 50,000 towns, one plow is decayed since the 1 Hen. VII,</small>

The *whiche .l. thousande plowes, euerye ploughe were able to mainteine .vi. persons: That is to saye, the man, the wyfe, and fower other in his house, lesse and more. .l. thousande plowes, six persons to euery plough, draweth to the nomber of thre hundred thousand persons were wont to haue meate, drynke, and rayment, vprysing and down lyinge, paying skot and

<small>[* sign: B. iij.] which 50,000 plows represent a loss of 300,000 persons,</small>

<small>who paid scot and</small>

lot to God, & to the Kyng. And now they haue nothynge, but goeth about in England from dore to dore, and axe theyr almose for Goddes sake. And because they will not begge, some of them doeth steale, and then they be hanged, and thus the Realme doeth decay, and by none other wayes els, as we do thynke. Besechynge your Hyghnes (of your moste noble grace) and honourable lordshyppes, the premisses tenderly considered before you in examinacion vpon the premisses, that we may haue a remedy in this behalf. And we shall dayely praye for the conseruacion of your Highnes, and for your ful noble lordshyppes.

Finis.

¶ Imprinted at London in
Pouls churche yearde
at the sygne of Saynct
Austen by Heugh Syn-
gelton[1].

---

[1] Dibdin's *Ames* gives dates for Singleton from 1553 (or 1550 according to Herbert's notes), and says that Singleton died in 1592-3. The date of the present tract cannot therefore be earlier than 1550, or later than 1553, when Edward VI, to whose Council it is evidently addrest, died.—F.

NOTES.

p. 36. *Six Articles.*—These celebrated Articles are found in the "Bloody Statute," 31 Hen. VIII. cap. 14. They run :—1. That in the most blessed Sacrament of the Altar, by the strength and efficacy of Christ's mighty word (it being spoken by the priest) is present really under the form of bread and wine, the natural body and blood of our Saviour Jesus Christ, conceived of the Virgin Mary ; and that after the consecration there remains no substance of bread or wine, nor any other substance, but the Substance of Christ God and Man.

2. That the communion in both kinds is not necessary *ad salutem* by the law of God to all persons : and that it is to be believed and not doubted of, but that in the flesh under the form of bread is the very blood, and with the blood under the form of wine is the very flesh as well apart as though they were both together.

3. That priests, after the order of priesthood received as afore, may not marry by the law of God.

4. That vows of chastity or widowhead by man or woman made to God advisedly, ought to be observed by the law of God ; and that it exempteth them from other liberties of Christian people, which without that they might enjoy.

5. That it is meet and necessary that private Masses be continued and admitted in the King's English Church and congregation, as whereby good Christian people ordering themselves accordingly, do receive both godly and goodly consolation and benefit; and it is agreeable also to God's law.

6. That auricular confession is expedient and necessary to be retained and continued, used and frequented in the Church of God.—*Statutes at Large*, ii. 149, ed. 1811. Commissions were issued to the Archbishops, Bishops, &c., to execute the Act, and to them powers were given to take and burn books containing matters contrary to it. The Act was to be read quarterly in all churches.

p. 62. *Outbreak in* 1536-7.—On the 2nd of October, 1536, when the Ecclesiastical Commissioners were to hold their visitation at Louth, they found a great body of peasantry in arms, clamouring for their holidays; and proclaiming that they were gathered together for the maintenance of the faith, which was about to be destroyed. So far from Henry having finished his "godly purpose without bloudshede" of his "poore commones" (p. 63) he "wrote to Norfolk on the 22nd February, to 'cause such dreadful execution to be done upon a good number of the inhabitants of every town, village, and hamlet, that have offended in this rebellion, as they may be a fearful spectacle to all others hereafter that would practise any like matter.' A priest and a butcher at Windsor were hanged for expressing sympathy with the Northern rebels."—*Knight's Crown Hist. of Eng.*, p. 198, 200.

pp. 64—68. *The Bible.*—It was in 1536 that the Vicar-general's injunctions directed every parish priest to place a copy of the whole Bible in his church. These copies were all based upon Tyndal's translation. The bishops, although they had undertaken to supply a version which should suit Catholic orthodoxy, left their work untouched. In 1539 Taverner's Bible appeared. This contained a summary of things in Holy Scripture. "The priesthood was denied; masses and purgatory were ignored; the sacraments were described as nothing but outward signs." This led to the sale of unauthorized editions being forbidden, and after some discussion " a temporary limitation was imposed, perhaps wisely, upon its indiscriminate use." "It was wrangled over in alehouses and tap-rooms. It was disfigured 'in rhymes, printed ballads, plays, songs, and other fantasies.' Scandalous brawls and controversies disgraced the churches where it was placed for the people to read."— *Froude*, iv. 288—291. In the 34 and 35 Hen. VIII. cap. 1, the Bible was forbidden to be read in English in any church. Women, artificers, prentices, journeymen, servingmen, husbandmen, and labourers, might read the New Testament in English. Nothing was to be taught or maintained contrary to the King's Instructions.—*Stat. at Large*, ii. 201.

p. 67. *Thomas Cromwell, Earl of Essex.*—It was "with the private connivance of Cromwell" that "other editions" of the Bible than those authorized were put in circulation (*Froude*, iv. 289), and this was not forgotten when he stood attainted of treason. Not only was he accused of having "been the most corrupt traitor and deceiver of the king and the crown that had ever been known in his whole reign," but it was alleged that " he being also a heretic, had dispersed many erroneous books among the king's subjects, [the Bible probably being one,] particularly some that were contrary to the belief of the sacrament." On the day of his beheading, 28th July, 1540, Henry married Catherine Howard.[1] Six years later one of the very party, to serve which he had risked (and lost) so much, was found to brand him as " a traytoure!"

p. 69. *Boulogne.*—On the 18th of September, 1544, Henry made his solemn entry into Boulogne.—*Knight*, p. 211. *See also* Froude, iv. 352.

[1] Knight's Crown Hist. of Eng., p. 206.

NOTES.   105

p. 75. *The Holy Maid of Kent.* Elizabeth Barton.—" About the time of Easter, in the seventeenth yeere of the Reigne of King Henrie the Eight, it hapned a certaine maiden . . . . servant to one Thomas Kob . . . to bee touched with a great infirmitie in her bodie, which did ascend at divers times up into her throte, and swelled greatly" (*Lambarde's Perambulation*, p. 170, rep.). Her history is well known. "In the ende her dissimulation was deciphered, her Popish comforters were bewraied, the deceived people were well satisfied, these daungerous deceivers were worthely executed, and the Devill their Master was quite and cleane confounded."—*Ib.* p. 175.

p. 75. *The Rood of Kent* was at Boxley. It is thus described by Lambarde (p. 205) :—" It chaunced (as the tale is) that upon a time, a cunning Carpenter of our countrie was taken prisoner in the warres betweene us and Fraunce, who (wanting otherwise to satisfie for his raunsome, and having good leysure to devise for his deliveraunce) thought it best to attempt some curious enterprise, within the compasse of his owne Art and skill, to make himselfe some money withall : And therefore, getting togither fit matter for his purpose, he compacted of wood, wyer, paste and paper, a Roode of such exquisite arte and excellencie, that it not onely matched in comelynesse and due proportion of the partes the best of the common sorte ; but in straunge motion, variety of gesture, and nimblenes of ioints, passed al other that before had been seene : the same being able to bow down and lift up it selfe, to shake and stirre the handes and feete, to nod the head, to rolle the eies, to wag the chaps, to bende the browes, and finally to represent to the eie, both the proper motion of each member of the body, and also a lively, expresse, and significant shew of a well contented or displeased minde : byting the lippe, and gathering a frowning, froward, and disdainful face, when it would pretend offence : and shewing a most milde, amyable, and smyling cheere and countenaunce, when it woulde seeme to be well pleased."

p. 91. *Queen Catherine Howard.*—In 1541, Henry solemnly offered thanksgiving for the happiness he found in the society of this his Fifth Queen. On the 12th of February, 1542, she and lady Rochford were executed.

GENERAL INDEX.

ABBEY lands, how bestowed, 80.
Abbeys have become "caves of beasts," 64.
Allen, Dr, his conduct, 12, 18.
Apparel, costliness of, 52.
Archery decays, 100.
Articles, the Six, 36, 103.
Ass, the man who would make one dance, 68.

Beef is dearer, 97.
Beggars, 8.
Beggars, the Supplication of, given to the King, vi; cast about London streets, x; referred to, 61.
Bible, the, may be taken from the laity, 37; by whom it might be read, 64; to be placed in churches, 67; to be called in, 68; translation of, 69.
Bishoprics, how bestowed, 34.
Bishops' negligence, the consequences of, 37, 40, 41, 53; possessions of, 47; their worldly business, 48; how they use their riches, 49, 50; the offices they seek, 51, 54, 55; they must be taken away, 56; how they might be tested, 83.
Boleyn, Lady Anne, gives Fish's book to the King, vi.
Books in English forbidden, x; list of, xii; contrary to the Six Articles to be burnt, 36, 103.
Boulogne, capture of, 69, 104.
Brinklow, R., may have written *Supplications*, xiii
Buckinghamshire, decay in, 96, 99.
Bygod, Sir F., quoted on idleness in abbeys, 15, *note*.

Cattle-breeding neglected, 96.
Celibacy, 75.
Chaplain, the, with numerous livings, 78.
Chaplains, the numbers of, 29, 30; privileges of, 76.
Children can't be sent to school, 80.
Church, the, what it teaches, 74.
Clergy, abuse and treatment of the, xv; conduct of the, 1; gains of the, 2; ignorance of, 21, 27, 32, 33; cause of ignorance in others, 23, 35; fees received by the, 87; what they would tithe if they dare, 87; sevenths paid to, 88.
Commission to forbid the reading of English books, x.
Corn, deficiency of, 95.
Cottages go down, 79, 97.
Craftsmen and labourers, lamentation of, 101.

GENERAL INDEX.   107

Cromwell, Thomas, Earl of Essex, 67, 104.

Dates of 2nd and 3rd *Supplications*, xiii.

Dead, prayers for the, 44, 45.

Drunkenness, 53.

Eggs are dearer, 97.

Elyot and Robinson introduced to the King, viii.

English, service in, 89.

Fashions, extravagant, xv, 52.

Fees received by the clergy, 87.

Fish, Simon, the story of, vi; Wood's account of, xiii; introduced to the King, vii; dies of the plague, vii.

Fish's wife persecuted by Sir T. More, vii.

Friars and monks, numbers of, 2, 4, 42; the money and property they receive, 3, 4, 9, 42; their rebellious conduct, 4, 5.

Frith's answer to Sir T. More's *Purgatory*, x.

Heresy, men accused of, 8.

Horsey, Dr, his conduct in Hunne's case, 12.

Hospitality, decay of, 99.

Hospitals are abused, 13.

Howard, Queen Catherine, referred to, 91, 105.

Hunne, Richard, his life and death, 9, 12, 16.

Kent, the Holy Maid and winking Rood of, 75, 104, 105.

Kine kept in every house, 99.

King, the tokens of his end, 81.

Kings, how they have bestowed bishopricks 34.

Latin, service in, 89.

Laws, good, made, 25.

Lawyers, plenty of, 51.

Learning in England, 21; what sort of, 23.

London, a grievous charge on, 84.

Losses sustained by the country by the change in farming, xvi, 97—100.

Maid of Kent, the Holy, 75, 104.

Masses paid for, but unsaid, 14.

Meat, white, is dearer, 97.

Moddys, Edmund, the King's footman, talks of religion and the new books, viii.

Monks, their lust, 6, 9, 15; ought to be married, 7; their prayers, 9, 10; how they ought to be treated, 14, 15; their idleness, 15, *note;* possessions of, 61.

Monks and nuns "weeded out," 62.

More, Sir T., his *Supplycacyon of Soulys*, v, viii; answered by Frith, x; his *Utopia*, ix; persecutes Fish's wife, vii.

Mortmain, statute of, 9, 12.

Music, Church, 75.

Mutton is dearer, 97.

Non-residence and pluralities, 28, 29.

Northamptonshire, decay in, 96, 99.

Oxfordshire, decay in, 96, 98.

Parishes and parish churches, number of, in England, 2, 101.

Pater noster, No penny, no, 87.

Patronage, abuses of, 77.

Patrons are negligent, 27; and bestow livings on the undeserving, 35; warned, 31, 33; their duties, 38.

GENERAL INDEX.

Plow, how many persons one would keep, 98.
Plows, more to be kept, 100; how many less, 101.
Poor, numbers of, 8; ought to be relieved, 44; the, how to be provided for, 70; the, were better off under the old condition of things, 79; the, how they are oppressed—some beg, some steal, some are hanged, 79; driven to beg or steal, 98, 102.
Population, checks to increase of, 6, 15.
Poultry scarcer, 98, 100.
Poverty of the people, xv; 1, 43, 61.
Preaching, the want of, and its results, 26.
Pride, 53.
Proverbs, six, 95, 96.
Purgatory, 10, 45.

Rebellion referred to, 64, 103.
Rents are raised, 79.
Rich, the conduct of the, xv.
Robinson and Elyot have an interview with the King, viii.
Roo, M., his play or interlude, vi.
Rood of Kent, the, 75, 105.
Roy, William, v, *note*.

Sacrament, people beg to pay for the, 5.
School, why children cannot be sent to, 80.
Schools should be founded out of abbey funds, 44.

Scriptures, ignorance of the, 22.
Service in Latin and English, 89.
Sevenths paid to clergy, 88.
Sheep and sheepmasters, 95, 96.
Sheep Tract, subject of, xvi; date of, 103.
Shepherds and archery, 100.
Simony, 82.
Six Articles, books contrary to, to be burnt, 36, 103.
Supplications, authorship of, xiii; subjects discussed in, xiv.
Swearing, 53.

Tenants of Abbey-lands, how treated, 80.
Testament, the New, forbidden, x, xi; translations of the, 67, 104.
Thieves, 8.
Tillage not attended to, 96.
Tithes, origin and history of, 70—74; payable on sheep dying of rot, 85.
Tonstall's prohibition of English New Testaments, x.
Traditions of the Church, 74.
Tramps, then and now, xvii, *note*.

Unemployed, the numbers of, then, xvii.
Usury, 82, 84.
Utopia of Sir T. More, ix.

Vice is rampant, 82.
Vices which are prevalent, 53.

Wood's account of Fish, xiii.
Wool is dearer, 97.

GLOSSARIAL INDEX.

NOTE. B. = Bailey's Dictionary; P. = Kersey's Phillips; Bp Bale = The Select Works of Bp. Bale, Parker Society; P.P. = Promptorium Parvulorum; H. = Halliwell's Arch. Dict.

My best thanks are due to the Rev. Dr Rock and the Rev. W. W. Skeat for their valuable assistance in the explanation of certain words in this Glossary.

ADDYOTE, 47, to give over to.

Aduaylable, 8, available.

Adulterine, 92, adulterate, counterfeit, corrupt.

Alckmist, 77, alchemist.

Amners, 34, almoners.

Artchers, 100, archers.

Artillary, 100, artillery, the art of shooting with bows and arrows.

Assityng, 2, to ascite, to call, to summon.

Attender, 96, to attend to.

Auncientie, 9, antiquity. *Antiquitie: auncientie. Cooperi Thesaurus*, in v. *antiquitas*.

A wiles, 68. ? In the mean time.

Axe, 101, ask.

Bedemen, 13. "Bedes men, alms-men, who pray'd for their founders and benefactors." *P. Bede* (A.S.), a prayer. "Your *bedman*, & seruantt to þe vttermust off my poor power, Andrew Boorde." *Furnivall's Andrew Boorde's Dyetary*, p. 62. "And the *bedeman* shall pray for the soul of the dead." *Toulmin Smith's English Gilds*, p. 230.

Bloudsupper, 5, a murderer, a bloodsucker. "Poor creatures that should be killed by these unsaciate *blood-soupers* for his truth's sake." *Bp Bale*, p. 324.

Bopipe, 68, bo-peep. "Some of the byshoppes at your injunctyons slepe, Some laugh and go bye, and some can play *boo pipe*." *Bale's Kynge Johan*, p. 97.

Brenninge, 41, burning.

Bruit, 64, brute.

Bryres, 56, briers.

Buggery, 63, "the coupling of one man with another, or of man or woman with a brute beast." P.

Bumme court, 48, a court which took cognizance of certain vices.

By, set by, 97, thought much of.

Cannebes, 75, canopies. "*Cannabie, canabie*, a corruption of canopy." *Jamieson*: who adds that it is used in Inventories. "*Canopeum, reticulum subtile factum de canabo*. The Canope alluded to in the Promptorium was very probably the *Umbraculum* under which the Sacred Host was carried in the

9 *

procession on Palm Sunday. Canapy to be borne over the sacrament." *P. P., note* 3, p. 60. Lat. *cannabis*, hemp. "Going processions with *canopy*, cross, and pix." Bp Bale, p. 524.

Carp, 88, talk, or speak.

Catyuite, 23, captivity.

Chaplaynes, 42. "Rydynge Chaplaynes"?

Church ales, 41; a church ale was a feast in commemoration of the dedication of a church.

Cocke of haye, 65, "a conical heap of hay." *H.*

Coelginers, 66. Bailey has "coeliginous," but whether the "Coelginers" were a "heaven-born" sect or what they were I don't know. Cp. "Then was there an infinite table of . . . . . . sententioners and summists, of *colliginers* and canonists." Bp Bale, p. 350. Canon Rock suggests that the writer meant Culdees. "The Culdees were a sect of religious monks, remarkable for their religious exercises of preaching and praying." *B.*

Cohybyted, 25, hindered.

Commessacyon, 53, commessation, revelling.

Coopes, 75, Copes. "Cope, a sacred vestment which is directed by the Canons of the Reformed Church to be worn at the celebration of the communion in cathedral and collegiate church." *P. P., note* 2, p. 91.

Corporace, 75, "Corporasse, or corporalle. *Corporale.*" *P.P.* "The term corporas, *corporalis palla*, denotes a consecrated linen cloth folded and placed upon the altar in the service of the mass, beneath the sacred elements." *Ib. note* 3, p. 93. The corporal "is the name given to the linen cloth which is spread over the body (*corpus*), or consecrated bread, in the communion." *Hook's Church Dict.*, 9th ed. So that the corporas or corporal is placed *beneath* the Elements by the Roman Catholic, *over* them by the Protestant.

Couentes, 80, convents.

Counfortable, 28, comfortable.

Counforte, 28, comfort.

Covent, 27, convent.

Cream, 41, *Chrism.* Oil consecrated in the Romish and Greek churches by the bishop, and used in baptism, confirmation, orders, and extreme unction. "At the last crept in the worshipping of relics and shrines, with holy oil and *cream.*" Bp Bale, p. 320.

Crwetes, 75, cruets. "Crewet or crevet, a little vial, or narrow-mouth'd glass." *P.* "Copes, crosses, *cruets.*" Bp Bale, p. 259.

Cukkoldrie, 6, the act of adultery.

Cure, 29, care.

Dasshed, 8, condemned, confounded. "The gentlemen were *dashed* by his earnestness." *Ginx's Baby*, p. 175.

Debities, 85, deputies. "These spiritual tyrants shall examine you . . . . and so deliver you up unto kings and *debities.*" Bp Bale, p. 6.

Demaner, 61, demeanour.

Demurante, 32, grave in behaviour.

Deplorate, 46, deplorable.

Dimitted, vii, dismissed, sent away.

Distayne, 81, to stain.

Dwe, 77, due.

Dome, 53, dumb.

Drafsacke, 15, a sack full of draf, a place of extreme wickedness. "Proving their traditions to be most vile *draff*, and most stinking dregs of sin." Bp Bale, p. 285.

GLOSSARIAL INDEX. 111

Effectuously, x, effectually, completely. "That Esay..... with all other prophets, warneth aforehand to follow concerning Christ and his church, this mystery declareth *effectuously* fulfilled." *Bp Bale*, p. 253.

Elbowhangers, 77, hangers-on, parasites.

Enmious, ix, inimical, hostile. "Enmy. *Inimicus, hostis, hostilitas.*" *P. P.*

Enmying, ix. *See above.*

Enprysonmente, 36, imprisonment.

Enterdite, 5, interdict.

Entermedlyng, xi, intermixing.

Eretik, 9, heretic.

Estatute, 30, statute.

Exquysytely, 22, exquisitely, accurately, with great exactness; minutely. "Exquisite, curious, choice; also exact, or carry'd on to the utmost height." *P.*

Externe, 91, external.

Felles, 85, fells, skins, or hides.

Fiftenes, 3, fifteenths.

Frayd, 84, afraid.

Fumish, viii, angry, fractious.

Fumishly, ix, angrily.

Galpe, 81, gape, gape after, to look forward to.

Gnatonical, 77, 89, gnat-like.

Goulafres, 10. See note, p. 10.

Gyldes, 75. "Gild, guild, or geld, A company of men united together, with laws and orders made among themselves." *P.* In the text it means the house in which a religious fraternity or gild lived.

Habilite, 65, ability, power, or authority.

Habitacle, 24, a dwelling or habitation. "And he shall finally sup with me and with him in the eternal *habitacle* of God .." *Bp Bale*, p. 296.

Holle, 50, whole.

Hyed, 50, hide.

Hylded, 85, skinned. *Hild*, to skin. *H.*

Illected, 6, enticed. "Illectus. Pleasantly prouoked, intised, tolled, allured." *Cooperi Thesaurus.*

Impe, 92, a shoot of a tree, a cutting, a bud. "He shall be called .... a lamb of Christ's fold, a sheep of his pasture, a branch of his vine, a member of his church, an *imp* of his kingdom." *Bp Bale,* p. 292. The same writer uses it in a bad sense: "O very *imps* of hell, and limbs of the devil!" p. 441.

Importune, 84, importunate.

Iorney, 71, journey.

Iote, 83, jot. "One *iote*, or one title of the law shal not scape." S. Mat. v. 18, *Genevan New Test.* 1557.

Iour, 92, your.

Ioywell, 39, jewel.

Kyre Eleyson, 69. Kyrie Eleison, the Greek of "Lord, have mercy" upon us.

Latward, 71. "Lateward, that is of the latter season." *P.*

Lazer, 77, leprous, afflicted with leprosy.

Leas, 80, lease.

Liripope, 84. The following is Mr Halliwell's note on this word: "*Liripoops.* An appendage to the ancient hood, consisting of long tails or tippets, passing round the neck, and hanging down before, reaching to the feet, and often jagged. The term is often jocularly used by writers of the 16th and 17th centuries. 'A lirripoop *vel* lerripoop, a silly empty creature, an old dotard.' *Milles, MS. Devon Gloss.* A priest was formerly jocularly termed a *lerry-cum-poop*. It seems to mean a trick or stratagem, in the *London Prodigal*, p. 111. 'And whereas thou takest the matter so farre in snuffe, I will teach thee thy *lyrripups* after another fashion than to be thus malepertlie cocking and billing with me, that am thy governour.' *Stanihurst*, p. 35. Theres a girle that knowes her *lerripoope*. *Lillie's Mother Bombie*, 1594." "I believe the scarf grew out of the fur tippet or almuce, or amess, not the *liripipe* of the hood." *Church Times*, 16 Dec., 1870, p. 536, col. 4.

Lobies, 14, looby, a silly awkward fellow. *H.*

Loutes, 15, clownish unmannerly fellows.

Lubbers, 15. "Abbey loutes or lubbers." Drudges, lazy drones. "Idul *abbey-lubbarys*, wych are apte to no thyng but ... only to ete and drynke." *England in Henry VIII's Time*, p. 131, ed. J. M. Cowper.

Lubricite, 7, lubricity, incontinency. See *Lubricus*, Cooperi Thesaurus.

Lyuelycke, 66, lively, living.

Maiheme, 8. "Maihem or Mahim, (F.) maim, wound, hurt." *P.*

Morowe mas, 42. Morrow Mass. I am indebted to Canon Rock for the following:—"Time out of mind and while the Anglo-Saxons ruled, there used to be in every monastery, cathedral, and large church, in this land, two altars in every chancel : one, the high or large altar; the other, a smaller altar, not always but usually at the back of this larger altar. Every morning at dawn, and at the end of matins, a mass was sung or said at the smaller altar, and the monk or priest who celebrated it was termed the morrow-mass priest; and the altar itself was named the morrow Mass Altar." "The morrow masse awter" of Faversham had, in the 4th Henry VIII. "Imprimis. A chisebyll of grene damaske with lyones of golde with apparel for the preest. It. A masse boke preynted. It. 2 cruetts of pewter. It. 2 kandylstykks and a small of laton standing upon brods herse." *Jacob's Faversham*, p. 164. And *Thomas Sterkey* of Faversham gave, in 1525, "to the *morrow masse* aultar every weeke a penny after my decese the space of one whole yere." *Lewis's Fun. Mon. in the Church of Faversham*, p. 37.

Mortwaries, 85, mortuaries. "Mortuary, in the English ecclesiastical law, is a gift left by a man at his death to his parish church, in recompence of personal tithes omitted to be paid in his lifetime. By 21 Hen. VIII. c. 6, mortuaries were commuted into money payments." *Hook's Ch. Dict.*

Mought, 5, might.

Muncke pencyons, 42, ? Monk pensioners.

Murmuracyon, 26, murmur, or murmuring.

Mysse, 78, a wrong, that which is amiss.

Nasturcium, ix, the herb nose-smart.

Noble, 80, a coin of the value of 6s. 8d. "And in thys yere (1527) begane the golde to ryse, as the angell *nobyll* at vijs. and in November after it was made vijs. vjd." *Grey Friars' Chron.*, p. 33. The angel also was of the value of 6s. 8d.

GLOSSARIAL INDEX. 113

But when "a phisician called Doctour Nicholas," received "xx Angellis, vij li. x. s." the angel was worth 7s. 6d. *Furnivall's Andrew Boorde*, p. 49, *note* 1.

Obeisant, 81, obedient.

Obeysaunce, 90, obedience.

Other, 46, either.

Outwarde, 33, outer, St Matt. viii. 12. Comp. "Thou shalt be thrown forth into *exterior* darkness, where shall be weeping." *Bp Bale*, p. 294.

Palme trees, 78. The Sallow, *salix caprea*, is commonly known in the Midland counties as the Palm.
"For look here, what 1 found on a *palm*-tree."
As You Like It, iii. 2.
"Ye leaning *palms*, that seem to look
Pleased o'er your image in the brook."
Clare's Rural Life, p. 62.

Pax, 75. A small tablet of silver, or some fit material, often very elaborately ornamented, by means of which the kiss of peace was, in the mediæval Church, circulated through the congregation. "Crucifixes.... borne aloft in their gaddings abroad, with the religious occupyings of their *paxes*, cruets, and jewels which be of silver." *Bp Bale*, p. 526.

Pewling, viii, ix, x. "To pule, to piep or cry as chickens and young birds do. To whine, to cry, to whimper." B.
"To speak *puling*, like a beggar at Hallowmas."
Two Gent. Ver. ii. 1.
"A wretched *puling* fool, A whining mammet."
Rom. & Jul. iii. 5.

Persequution, 73, persecution.

Personagyes, 34, parsonages. "So is there in *personages*, some sente from Christ as shepherds to fede, and some from the deuyll as theues to deuoure." *Lever's Sermons*, p. 66, Arber's reprint.

Pettyt, 87, petty, little, small, paltry.

Pixes, 75. Pyx, the vessel or box in which the Host is kept. Irreverently called "god-boxes" by Bp Bale, p. 527.

Pours, 63, powers, authorities.

Prescripte, 41, prescribed, appointed. "The dwellers of the earth ... practised worshippings besides the *prescripte* rules of God's word." *Bp Bale*, p. 495.

Prist, 90, priest.

Prodicessours, 77, predecessors.

Prophanate, xi, to profane.

Prossession, 69, ? procession.

Prystishe, 45, priestish.

Pue, 67, pew.

Pyed, 79, black and white, particoloured. "These [freres of the Pye] would appear to be not very different from the Carmelites; they were called *Pied Friars* from their dress being a mixture of black and white, like a magpie." *Pierce the Ploughmans Crede*, ed. Skeat, p. 35. "The Pied Friars had but one house, viz. at Norwich. We find the expression 'Fratrum, quos *Freres Pye* veteres appellabant' in Thom. Walsingham, Hist. Anglicana, vol. i. p. 182; ed. H. T. Riley. See also Notes and Queries, 4 S. ii. 496." *Additional Note to the same*.

Pynfolde, viii, a place of confinement.

Quest, 9, inquest, a jury of citizens.

Realyfe, 70, relief.

Renomed, 82, renowned.

SUPPLICATION. 8

Reuaile, 69, reveal.

Royalme, 78, realm.

Salue, 28, to apply salve to, to heal.

Scala celi, 41, Scala Cœli, the name given to "a vision of St Bernard's, who, while celebrating a funereal mass, saw the souls for whom he was praying going up to heaven by a ladder." Sometimes the term "is used merely as one of mystical figurative names of the Madonna." *Political and Rel. Poems*, xxvii.

Scase, 29, scarce. See *England in Hen. VIII's Time*, scaseness, p. 223.

Seased, 80 (Law term), seized of, possessed of.

Sence, 41, cense, to perfume with incense.

Sensoures, 75, censers.

Serpentical, 74, serpent-like, devilish.

Shauelings, 41. A term of contempt for a priest. "This Babylonish whore, or disguised synagogue of *shorelings*, sitteth upon many waters or peoples." *Bp Bale*, p. 494. *Shavelings* of prodigious beastliness in lecherous living under the colour of chastity. *Ib.* p. 497.

Shepe, 75, ? ship. "Schyppe, vesselle to put yn rychel (incense)" *P. P.* "*Acerra*, a *schyp* for censse," Nominale MS. xv. Cent. quoted by Halliwell. "He gave a senser, and a *shyp* of clene syluer, *argento puro.*" *Horman, P. P.* p. 80, note 6. Sir T. More uses the word, but the reference I have not at hand. Canon Rock tells me he thinks *sheep* is meant. He says, "It was usual in those times for people having nothing better to bestow in charity, to give certain animals to the church that therewith some money might arise, to be expended for charitable purposes: cows, for instance, that their milk, butter, and cheese might produce sums for charity; and sheep for the wool they produced, to be sold for the like purpose. The ship for incense is not a thimble, but an oblong shallow kind of box for holding incense. This appliance is now called 'an incense boat,' and in Latin is known as the *navicula*, because shaped in the form of one, but without any mast."

Skanter, 96, scarcer.

Skantite, 95, scarceness.

Skot and lot, 98, "a customary contribution laid upon all subjects according to their ability." *B.* "Every freeholder is bound to be a partaker in *lot*, which is liability to hold office, and in *scot*, which means contribution to taxes and other charges." *Riley's Mem. of London*, p. 601, quoted in *Smith's English Gilds*, p. 474.

Sloughtfully, 3, ? cruelly, murderously.

Sparcled, vi, enlightened, illuminated.

Steare, 24, 63, stir.

Sternelynges, 64, starvelings; lean, hungry-looking persons.

Strawne, x, strewn, scattered.

Sumner, 17, summoner. See note, p. 17.

Swynescotes, 78, pig-sties.

Swynged, 69, repeated frequently and loudly.

Tapurs, 75, tapers.

Thouchyng, 96, touching.

Towardnes, 81. "Child of great towardness," child of great promise.

Trentalles, 41, Trental, a service of thirty masses for the dead, usually celebrated on as many different days. "On þe morwe to seie a *trent* of masses." *Smith's English Gilds*, p. 8. "Pour out your *trental* masses, spew out your commendations." *Bp Bale*, p. 330. See *St Gregory's Trental*, Pol. Rel. and Love Poems.

Vmbermente, 96, number. Vmber, number. *H.*

Vnaxed, 8, unasked.

Vndoutely, 65, undoubtedly.

Voult safe, 85, vouchsafe. Another form of the word is *withsave*. "For unto them only are his heavenly verities known, to whom he *withsaveth* to open them." *Bp Bale*, p. 473.

Vre, 51, ure, use.

Vtylite, 3, utility.

Wayne, 23, vain.

Warmoll, 9. See note, p. 9. Mr Skeat says: "*Warnmall*. I know nothing of it, and can only guess. It may be *warn*, to admonish, and *mall*. But what is *mall?* It can hardly be Fr. *mal*. It can hardly be *Mall* or *Moll*, a common name for frail ones. Nor am I satisfied with a friend's guess that the word is *warn-'em-all!* It's too clever. And as if to make that which is dark darker, I find A.S. *worn-mælum* (spelt *wearn-mælum* in Bosworth) means *by companies.* Cf. O.E. *flockmel*, by flocks, and *piece-meal*, by pieces."

Weyte, 97, white.

Wringyng, 77. "To wrest... to *wring*... to force the sense of a passage or author." *P.*

Wyllouse, 78, willows.

Wyte, ix, blame, reproach.

Yie, 1, eye.

Yower, 75, ewer.

Ypochrise, 11, hypocrisy.

Ypochrite, 11, hypocrites.

The manufacturer's authorised representative in the EU for product safety is Oxford University Press España S.A. of El Parque Empresarial San Fernando de Henares, Avenida de Castilla, 2 - 28830 Madrid (www.oup.es/en or product.safety@oup.com). OUP España S.A. also acts as importer into Spain of products made by the manufacturer.
Printed and bound by CPI Group (UK) Ltd, Croydon, CR0 4YY
23/03/2026
02076308-0007